P9-BXZ-480

BIBLE STORIES
FOR YOUNG ONES

CHILDREN OF GOD

*An illustrated Bible storybook on
the amazing deeds of the Apostles*

THOMAS NELSON PUBLISHERS
Nashville

This storybook contains the text of the Acts of the Apostles, the book of the Bible that describes how the first Christians took the good news about Jesus Christ to the people of many nations, to tell them how they also could become children of God.

The Bible used is the Contemporary English Version, an accurate translation of the original texts into natural, current English that readers of all ages can understand and enjoy.

The stories are illustrated by beautiful new watercolor paintings by artist Natalie Carabetta.

Whether they are being read to or are reading the stories themselves, children will be delighted with the vivid narration of these events from the exciting early days of the church.

Difficult phrases or passages are marked with a star (*) and are explained in *Notes* in the back of the book, where they are listed by page numbers.

CONTENTS

THE ACTS OF THE APOSTLES

(Acts 1.1-5)

Theophilus, I first wrote to you* about all that Jesus did and taught from the very first until he was taken up to heaven. But before he was taken up, he gave orders to the apostles he had chosen with the help of the Holy Spirit.

For forty days after Jesus had suffered and died, he proved in many ways that he had been raised from death. He appeared to his apostles and spoke to them about God's kingdom. While he was still with them, he said:

> Don't leave Jerusalem yet. Wait here for the Father to give you the Holy Spirit, just as I told you he has promised to do. John baptized with water, but in a few days you will be baptized with the Holy Spirit.

Jesus Is Taken to Heaven

(Acts 1.6-11)

While the apostles were still with Jesus, they asked him, "Lord, are you now going to give Israel its own king again?"*

Jesus said to them, "You don't need to know the time of those events that only the Father controls. But the Holy Spirit will come upon you and give you power. Then you will tell everyone about me in Jerusalem, in all Judea, in Samaria, and everywhere in the world." After Jesus had said this and while they were watching, he was taken up

into a cloud. They could not see him, but as he went up, they kept looking up into the sky.

Suddenly two men dressed in white clothes were standing there beside them. They said, "Why are you men from Galilee standing here and looking up into the sky? Jesus has been taken to heaven. But he will come back in the same way that you have seen him go."

Someone to Take the Place of Judas
(Acts 1.12-26)

The Mount of Olives was about half a mile from Jerusalem. The apostles who had gone there were Peter, John, James, Andrew, Philip, Thomas, Bartholomew, Matthew, James the son of Alphaeus, Simon, known as the Eager One,* and Judas the son of James.

After the apostles returned to the city, they went upstairs to the room where they had been staying.

The apostles often met together and prayed with a single purpose in mind.* The women and Mary the mother of Jesus would meet with them, and so would his brothers. One day there were about a hundred and twenty of the Lord's followers meeting together, and Peter stood up to speak to them. He said:

> My friends, long ago by the power of the Holy
> Spirit, David said something about Judas, and what

he said has now happened. Judas was one of us and had worked with us, but he brought the mob to arrest Jesus. Then Judas bought some land with the money he was given for doing that evil thing. He fell headfirst into the field. His body burst open, and all his insides came out. When the people of Jerusalem found out about this, they called the place Akeldama, which in the local language means "Field of Blood."

In the book of Psalms David said,

"Leave his house empty,
and don't let anyone
live there."

It also says,

"Let someone else
have his job."

So we need someone else to help us tell others that Jesus has been raised from death. He must also

be one of the men who was with us from the very beginning. He must have been with us from the time the Lord Jesus was baptized by John until the day he was taken to heaven.

Two men were suggested: one of them was Joseph Barsabbas, known as Justus, and the other was Matthias. Then they all prayed, "Lord, you know what everyone is like! Show us the one you have chosen to be an apostle and to serve in place of Judas, who got what he deserved." They drew names, and Matthias was chosen to join the group of the eleven apostles.

The Coming of the Holy Spirit
(Acts 2.1-13)

On the day of Pentecost* all the Lord's followers were together in one place. Suddenly there was a noise from heaven like the sound of a mighty wind! It filled the house where they were meeting. Then they saw what looked like fiery tongues moving in all directions, and a tongue came and settled on each person there. The Holy Spirit took control of everyone, and they began speaking whatever languages the Spirit let them speak.

Many religious Jews from every country in the world were living in Jerusalem. And when they heard this noise,

a crowd gathered. But they were surprised, because they were hearing everything in their own languages. They were excited and amazed, and said:

Don't all these who are speaking come from Galilee? Then why do we hear them speaking our very own languages? Some of us are from Parthia, Media, and Elam. Others are from Mesopotamia, Judea, Cappadocia, Pontus, Asia, Phrygia, Pamphylia, Egypt, parts of Libya near Cyrene, Rome, Crete, and Arabia. Some of us were born Jews, and others of us have chosen to be Jews. Yet we all hear them using our own languages to tell the wonderful things that God has done.

Everyone was excited and confused. Some of them even kept asking each other, "What does all this mean?"

Others made fun of the Lord's followers and said, "They are drunk."

Peter Speaks to the Crowd

(Acts 2.14-42)

Peter stood with the eleven apostles and spoke in a loud and clear voice to the crowd:

Friends and everyone else living in Jerusalem,

listen carefully to what I have to say! You are wrong to think that these people are drunk. After all, it is only nine o'clock in the morning. But this is what God had the prophet Joel say,

"When the last days come,
I will give my Spirit
      to everyone.
Your sons and daughters
      will prophesy.
Your young men
      will see visions,
and your old men
      will have dreams.
In those days I will give
      my Spirit to my servants,
both men and women,
      and they will prophesy.

I will work miracles
      in the sky above
and wonders
      on the earth below.
There will be blood and fire
      and clouds of smoke.
The sun will turn dark,
and the moon
      will be as red as blood
before the great

and wonderful day
of the Lord appears.
Then the Lord
will save everyone
who asks for his help."
Now, listen to what I have to say about Jesus
from Nazareth. God proved that he sent Jesus to you
by having him work miracles, wonders, and signs. All
of you know this. God had already planned and
decided that Jesus would be handed over to you. So
you took him and had evil men put him to death on a
cross. But God set him free from death and raised
him to life. Death could not hold him in its power.
What David said are really the words of Jesus,
"I always see the Lord
near me,
and I will not be afraid
with him at my right side.
Because of this,
my heart will be glad,
my words will be joyful,
and I will live in hope.
The Lord won't leave me
in the grave.
I am his holy one,
and he won't let
my body decay.
He has shown me
the path to life,
and he makes me glad
by being near me."
My friends, it is right for me to speak to you
about our ancestor David. He died and was buried,

and his tomb is still here. But David was a prophet, and he knew that God had made a promise he would not break. He had told David that someone from his own family would someday be king.

David knew this would happen, and so he told us that Christ would be raised to life. He said that God would not leave him in the grave or let his body decay. All of us can tell you that God has raised Jesus to life!

Jesus was taken up to sit at the right side* of God, and he was given the Holy Spirit, just as the Father had promised. Jesus is also the one who has given the Spirit to us, and that is what you are now seeing and hearing.

David didn't go up to heaven. So he wasn't talking about himself when he said, "The Lord told my Lord to sit at his right side, until he made my Lord's enemies into a footstool for him." Everyone in Israel should then know for certain that God has made Jesus both Lord and Christ, even though you put him to death on a cross.

When the people heard this, they were very upset. They asked Peter and the other apostles, "Friends, what shall we do?"

Peter said, "Turn back to God! Be baptized in the name of Jesus Christ, so that your sins will be forgiven. Then you will be given the Holy Spirit. This promise is for you and your children. It is for everyone our Lord God will choose, no matter where they live."

Peter told them many other things as well. Then he said, "I beg you to save yourselves from what will happen to all these evil people." On that day about three thousand believed his message and were baptized. They spent their time learning from the apostles, and they were like family to each other. They also broke bread* and prayed together.

Life among the Lord's Followers
(Acts 2.43-47)

Everyone was amazed by the many miracles and wonders that the apostles worked. All the Lord's followers often met together, and they shared everything they had. They would sell their property and possessions and give the money to whoever needed it. Day after day they met together in the temple. They broke bread* together in different homes and shared their food happily and freely, while praising God. Everyone liked them, and each day the Lord added to their group others who were being saved.

Peter and John Heal a Lame Man
(Acts 3.1-10)

The time of prayer* was about three o'clock in the afternoon, and Peter and John were going into the temple. A man who had been born lame was being carried to the temple door. Each day he was placed beside this door, known as the Beautiful Gate. He sat there and begged from the people who were going in.

The man saw Peter and John entering the temple, and he asked them for money. But they looked straight at him and said, "Look up at us!"

The man stared at them and thought he was going to get something. But Peter said, "I don't have any silver or gold! But I will give you what I do have. In the name of

Jesus Christ from Nazareth, get up and start walking."
Peter then took him by the right hand and helped him up.

At once the man's feet and ankles became strong, and
he jumped up and started walking. He went with Peter and
John into the temple, walking and jumping and praising
God. Everyone saw him walking around and praising God.
They knew that he was the beggar who had been lying
beside the Beautiful Gate, and they were completely
surprised. They could not imagine what had happened to
the man.

Peter Speaks in the Temple
(Acts 3.11-26)

While the man kept holding on to Peter and John,
the whole crowd ran to them in amazement at the place
known as Solomon's Porch.* Peter saw that a crowd had
gathered, and he said:

> Friends, why are you surprised at what has
> happened? Why are you staring at us? Do you think
> we have some power of our own? Do you think we
> were able to make this man walk because we are so

religious? The God that Abraham, Isaac, Jacob, and our other ancestors worshiped has brought honor to his Servant* Jesus. He is the one you betrayed. You turned against him when he was being tried by Pilate, even though Pilate wanted to set him free.

You rejected Jesus, who was holy and good. You asked for a murderer to be set free, and you killed the one who leads people to life. But God raised him from death, and all of us can tell you what he has done. You see this man, and you know him. He put his faith in the name of Jesus and was made strong. Faith in Jesus made this man completely well while everyone was watching.

My friends, I am sure that you and your leaders didn't know what you were doing. But God had his prophets tell that his Messiah would suffer, and now he has kept that promise. So turn to God! Give up your sins, and you will be forgiven. Then that time will come when the Lord will give you fresh strength. He will send you Jesus, his chosen Messiah. But Jesus must stay in heaven until God makes all things new, just as his holy prophets promised long ago.

Moses said, "The Lord your God will choose one of your own people to be a prophet, just as he chose me. Listen to everything he tells you. No one who disobeys that prophet will be one of God's people any longer."

Samuel and all the other prophets who came later also spoke about what is now happening. You are really the ones God told his prophets to speak to. And you were given the promise that God made to your ancestors. He said to Abraham, "All nations on earth will be blessed because of someone from your family." God sent his chosen Son* to you first, because God wanted to bless you and make each one of you turn away from your sins.

Peter and John Are Brought in Front of the Council
(Acts 4.1-22)

The apostles were still talking to the people, when some priests, the captain of the temple guard, and some Sadducees arrived. These men were angry because the apostles were teaching the people that the dead would be raised from death, just as Jesus had been raised from death. By now it was already late in the afternoon, and they arrested Peter and John and put them in jail for the night. But a lot of people who had heard the message

believed it. So by now there were about five thousand followers of the Lord.

The next morning the leaders, the elders, and the teachers of the Law of Moses met in Jerusalem. The high priest Annas was there, as well as Caiaphas, John, Alexander, and other members of the high priest's family. They brought in Peter and John and made them stand in the middle while they questioned them. They asked, "By what power and in whose name have you done this?"

Peter was filled with the Holy Spirit and told the nation's leaders and the elders:

You are questioning us today about a kind deed in which a crippled man was healed. But there is something we must tell you and everyone else in Israel. This man is standing here completely well because of the power of Jesus from Nazareth. You put Jesus to death on a cross, but God raised him to life. He is the stone that you builders thought was worthless, and now he is the most important stone of all. Only Jesus has the power to save! His name is the only one in all the world that can save anyone.

The officials were amazed to see how brave Peter and John were, and they knew that these two apostles were only ordinary men and not well educated. The officials were certain that these men had been with Jesus. But they could not deny what had happened. The man who had been healed was standing there with the apostles.

The officials commanded them to leave the council room. Then the officials said to each other, "What can we do with these men? Everyone in Jerusalem knows about this miracle, and we cannot say it didn't happen. But to keep this thing from spreading, we will warn them never again to speak to anyone about the name of Jesus." So they called the two apostles back in and told them that they must never, for any reason, teach anything about the name of Jesus.

Peter and John answered, "Do you think God wants us to obey you or to obey him? We cannot keep quiet about what we have seen and heard."

The officials could not find any reason to punish Peter and John. So they threatened them and let them go. The man who was healed by this miracle was more than forty years old, and everyone was praising God for what had happened.

Peter and Others Pray for Courage
(Acts 4.23-31)

As soon as Peter and John had been set free, they went back and told the others everything that the chief priests and the leaders had said to them. When the rest of the Lord's followers heard this, they prayed together and said:

Master, you created heaven and earth, the sea, and everything in them. And by the Holy Spirit you spoke to our ancestor David. He was your servant, and you told him to say:

"Why are all the Gentiles
    so furious?
Why do people
    make foolish plans?
The kings of earth
    prepare for war,
and the rulers
    join together

against the Lord
    and his Messiah."

Here in Jerusalem, Herod* and Pontius Pilate got together with the Gentiles and the people of Israel. Then they turned against your holy Servant* Jesus, your chosen Messiah. They did what you in your power and wisdom had already decided would happen.

Lord, listen to their threats! We are your servants. So make us brave enough to speak your message. Show your mighty power, as we heal people and work miracles and wonders in the name of your holy Servant* Jesus.

After they had prayed, the meeting place shook. They were all filled with the Holy Spirit and bravely spoke God's message.

Sharing Possessions

(Acts 4.32-37)

The group of followers all felt the same way about everything. None of them claimed that their belongings were their own, and they shared everything they had with each other. In a powerful way the apostles told everyone that the Lord Jesus was now alive. God greatly blessed his followers,* and no one went in need of anything. Everyone who owned land or houses would sell them and bring the money to the apostles. Then they would give the money to anyone who needed it.

Joseph was one of the followers who had sold a piece of property and brought the money to the apostles. He was a Levite from Cyprus, and the apostles called him Barnabas, which means, "one who encourages others."

Peter Condemns Ananias and Sapphira

(Acts 5.1-11)

Ananias and his wife Sapphira also sold a piece of property. But they agreed to cheat and keep some of the money for themselves.

So when Ananias took the rest of the money to the apostles, Peter said, "Why has Satan made you keep back some of the money from the sale of the property? Why have you lied to the Holy Spirit? The property was yours before you sold it, and even after you sold it, the money was still yours. What made you do such a thing? You didn't lie to people. You lied to God!"

As soon as Ananias heard this, he dropped dead, and everyone who heard about it was frightened. Some young men came in and wrapped up his body. Then they took it out and buried it.

Three hours later Sapphira came in, but she didn't know what had happened to her husband. Peter asked her, "Tell me, did you sell the property for this amount?"

"Yes," she answered, "that's the amount."

Then Peter said, "Why did the two of you agree to test the Lord's Spirit? The men who buried Ananias are by the door, and they will carry you out!" At once she fell at Peter's feet and died.

When the young men came back in, they found Sapphira lying there dead. So they carried her out and buried her beside her husband. All the church members were afraid, and so was everyone else who heard what had happened.

Peter's Unusual Power

(Acts 5.12-16)

The apostles worked many miracles and wonders among the people. All of the Lord's followers often met in

the part of the temple known as Solomon's Porch.* No one outside their group dared join them, even though everyone liked them very much.

Many men and women started having faith in the Lord. Then sick people were brought out to the road and placed on cots and mats. It was hoped that Peter would walk by, and his shadow would fall on them and heal them. A lot of people living in the towns near Jerusalem brought those who were sick or troubled by evil spirits, and they were all healed.

The Jewish Leaders Make Trouble for the Apostles
(Acts 5.17-42)

The high priest and all the other Sadducees who were with him became jealous. They arrested the apostles and put them in the city jail. But that night an angel from the Lord opened the doors of the jail and led the apostles out. The angel said, "Go to the temple and tell the people everything about this new life." So they went into the temple before sunrise and started teaching.

The high priest and his men called together their council, which included all of Israel's leaders. Then they ordered the apostles to be brought to them from the jail. The servants who were sent to the jail did not find the apostles. They returned and said, "We found the jail locked tight and the guards standing at the doors. But when we opened the doors and went in, we didn't find anyone there." The captain of the temple guard and the chief priests listened to their report, but they did not know what to think about it.

Just then someone came in and said, "Right now those men you put in jail are in the temple, teaching the people!" The captain of the temple police went with some of his servants and brought the apostles back. But they did not use force. They were afraid that the people might start throwing stones at them.

When the apostles were brought before the council, the high priest said to them, "We told you plainly not to teach in the name of Jesus. But look what you have done! You have been teaching all over Jerusalem, and you are trying to blame us for his death."

Peter and the apostles replied:

We don't obey people. We obey God. You killed Jesus by nailing him to a cross. But the God our ancestors worshiped raised him to life and made him our Leader and Savior. Then God gave him a place at his right side,* so that the people of Israel would turn back to him and be forgiven. We are here to tell you about all this, and so is the Holy Spirit, who is God's gift to everyone who obeys God.

When the council members heard this, they became so angry that they wanted to kill the apostles. But one of them was the Pharisee Gamaliel, a highly respected teacher. He ordered the apostles to be taken out of the room for a little while. Then he said to the council:

Men of Israel, be careful what you do with these two men. Not long ago Theudas claimed to be someone important, and about four hundred men joined him. But he was killed. All his followers were scattered, and that was the end of that.

Later, when the people of our nation were being counted, Judas from Galilee showed up. A lot of people followed him, but he was killed, and all his followers were scattered.

So I advise you to stay away from these men.

Leave them alone. If what they are planning is something of their own doing, it will fail. But if God is behind it, you cannot stop it anyway, unless you want to fight against God.

The council members agreed with what he said, and they called the apostles back in. They had them beaten with a whip and warned them not to speak in the name of Jesus. Then they let them go.

The apostles left the council and were happy, because God had considered them worthy to suffer for the sake of Jesus. Every day they spent time in the temple and in one home after another. They never stopped teaching and telling the good news that Jesus is the Messiah.

Seven Leaders for the Church
(Acts 6.1-7)

A lot of people were now becoming followers of the Lord. But some of the ones who spoke Greek started complaining about the ones who spoke Aramaic. They complained that the Greek-speaking widows were not given their share when the food supplies were handed out each day.

The twelve apostles called the whole group of followers together and said, "We should not give up preaching God's message in order to serve at tables.* My friends, choose seven men who are respected and wise and filled with God's Spirit. We will put them in charge of these things. We can spend our time praying and serving God by preaching."

This suggestion pleased everyone, and they began by choosing Stephen. He had great faith and was filled with the Holy Spirit. Then they chose Philip, Prochorus, Nicanor, Timon, Parmenas, and also Nicolaus, who worshiped with the Jewish people* in Antioch. These men were brought to the apostles. Then the apostles prayed and placed their hands on the men to show that they had been chosen to do this work. God's message spread, and many more people in Jerusalem became followers. Even a large number of priests put their faith in the Lord.

Stephen Is Arrested
(Acts 6.8-15)

God gave Stephen the power to work great miracles and wonders among the people. But some Jews from Cyrene and Alexandria were members of a group who called themselves "Free Men."* They started arguing with Stephen. Some others from Cilicia and Asia also argued with him. But they were no match for Stephen, who spoke with the great wisdom that the Spirit gave him. So they talked some men into saying, "We heard Stephen say terrible things against Moses and God!"

They turned the people and their leaders and the teachers of the Law of Moses against Stephen. Then they all grabbed Stephen and dragged him in front of the council.

Some men agreed to tell lies about Stephen, and they said, "This man keeps on saying terrible things about this holy temple and the Law of Moses. We have heard him claim that Jesus from Nazareth will destroy this place and change the customs that Moses gave us." Then all the council members stared at Stephen. They saw that his face looked like the face of an angel.

Stephen's Speech
(Acts 7.1-53)

The high priest asked Stephen, "Are they telling the truth about you?"

Stephen answered:

Friends, listen to me. Our glorious God appeared to our ancestor Abraham while he was still in Mesopotamia, before he had moved to Haran. God told him, "Leave your country and your relatives and go to a land that I will show you." Then Abraham left the land of the Chaldeans and settled in Haran.

After his father died, Abraham came and settled in this land where you now live. God didn't give him any part of it, not even a square foot. But God did promise to give it to him and his family forever, even though Abraham didn't have any children. God said that Abraham's descendants would live for a while in a foreign land. There they would be slaves and would be mistreated four hundred years. But he also said, "I will punish the nation that makes them slaves. Then later they will come and worship me in this place."

God said to Abraham, "Every son in each family must be circumcised to show that you have kept your agreement with me." So when Isaac was eight days old, Abraham circumcised him. Later, Isaac circumcised his son Jacob, and Jacob circumcised his twelve sons. These men were our ancestors.

Joseph was also one of our famous ancestors. His brothers were jealous of him and sold him as a slave to be taken to Egypt. But God was with him and rescued him from all his troubles. God made him so wise that the Egyptian king Pharaoh thought highly of him. Pharaoh even made Joseph governor over Egypt and put him in charge of everything he owned.

Everywhere in Egypt and Canaan the grain crops failed. There was terrible suffering, and our ancestors could not find enough to eat. But when Jacob heard that there was grain in Egypt, he sent our ancestors there for the first time. It was on their second trip that Joseph told his brothers who he was, and Pharaoh learned about Joseph's family.

Joseph sent for his father and his relatives. In all, there were seventy-five of them. His father went to Egypt and died there, just as our ancestors did. Later their bodies were taken back to Shechem and placed in the tomb that Abraham had bought from the sons of Hamor.

Finally, the time came for God to do what he had promised Abraham. By then the number of our people in Egypt had greatly increased. Another king was ruling Egypt, and he didn't know anything about Joseph. He tricked our ancestors and was cruel to them. He even made them leave their babies outside, so they would die.

During this time Moses was born. He was a very beautiful child, and for three months his parents took care of him in their home. Then when they were forced to leave him outside, the king's daughter found him and raised him as her own son. Moses was given the best education in Egypt. He was a strong man and a powerful speaker.

When Moses was forty years old, he wanted to help the Israelites because they were his own people. One day he saw an Egyptian mistreating one of them. So he rescued the man and killed the Egyptian. Moses thought the rest of his people would realize that God was going to use him to set them free. But they didn't understand.

The next day Moses saw two of his own people fighting, and he tried to make them stop. He said, "Men, you are both Israelites. Why are you so cruel to each other?"

But the man who had started the fight pushed Moses aside and asked, "Who made you our ruler and judge? Are you going to kill me, just as you killed that Egyptian yesterday?" When Moses heard this, he ran away to live in the country of Midian. His two sons were born there.

Forty years later, an angel appeared to Moses from a burning bush in the desert near Mount Sinai. Moses was surprised by what he saw. He went closer to get a better look, and the Lord said, "I am the God who was worshiped by your ancestors, Abraham, Isaac, and Jacob." Moses started shaking all over and didn't dare to look at the bush.

The Lord said to him, "Take off your sandals. The place where you are standing is holy. With my own eyes I have seen the suffering of my people in Egypt. I have heard their groans and have come down to rescue them. Now I am sending you back to Egypt."

This was the same Moses that the people rejected by saying, "Who made you our leader and judge?" God's angel had spoken to Moses from the bush. And God had even sent the angel to help Moses rescue the people and be their leader.

In Egypt and at the Red Sea and in the desert, Moses rescued the people by working miracles and wonders for forty years. Moses is the one who told the people of Israel, "God will choose one of your people to be a prophet, just as he chose me." Moses brought our people together in the desert, and the angel spoke to him on Mount Sinai. There he was given these life-giving words to pass on to us. But our ancestors refused to obey Moses. They rejected him and wanted to go back to Egypt.

The people said to Aaron, "Make some gods to lead us! Moses led us out of Egypt, but we don't know what's happened to him now." Then they made an idol in the shape of a calf. They offered sacrifices to the idol and were pleased with what they had done.

God turned his back on his people and left them. Then they worshiped the stars in the sky, just as it says in the Book of the Prophets, "People of Israel, you didn't offer sacrifices and offerings to me during those forty years in the desert. Instead, you carried the tent where the god Molech is worshiped, and you took along the star of your god Rephan. You made those idols and worshiped them. So now I will have you carried off beyond Babylonia."

The tent where our ancestors worshiped God was with them in the desert. This was the same tent that God had commanded Moses to make. And it was made like the model that Moses had seen. Later it was given to our ancestors, and they took it with them when they went with Joshua. They carried the tent along as they took over the land from those people that God had chased out for them. Our ancestors used this tent until the time of King David. He pleased God and asked him if he could build a house of worship for the people* of Israel. And it was finally King Solomon who built a house for God.*

But the Most High God does not live in houses made by humans. It is just as the prophet said, when he spoke for the Lord,

"Heaven is my throne,
and the earth
      is my footstool.
What kind of house
      will you build for me?
In what place will I rest?
      I have made everything."

You stubborn and hardheaded people! You are always fighting against the Holy Spirit, just as your ancestors did. Is there one prophet that your ancestors didn't mistreat? They killed the prophets who told about the coming of the One Who Obeys God.* And now you have turned against him and killed him. Angels gave you God's Law, but you still don't obey it.

Stephen Is Stoned to Death
(Acts 7.54—8.2)

When the council members heard Stephen's speech, they were angry and furious. But Stephen was filled with the Holy Spirit. He looked toward heaven, where he saw our glorious God and Jesus standing at his right side.* Then Stephen said, "I see heaven open and the Son of Man standing at the right side of God!"

The council members shouted and covered their ears. At once they all attacked Stephen and dragged him out of the city. Then they started throwing stones at him. The men

who had brought charges against him put their coats at the feet of a young man named Saul.*

As Stephen was being stoned to death, he called out, "Lord Jesus, please welcome me!" He kneeled down and shouted, "Lord, don't blame them for what they have done." Then he died.

Saul approved the stoning of Stephen. Some faithful followers of the Lord buried Stephen and mourned very much for him.

Saul Makes Trouble for the Church
(Acts 8.2-3)

At that time the church in Jerusalem suffered terribly. All of the Lord's followers, except the apostles, were scattered everywhere in Judea and Samaria. Saul started making a lot of trouble for the church. He went from house to house, arresting men and women and putting them in jail.

The Good News Is Preached in Samaria

(Acts 8.4-25)

The Lord's followers who had been scattered went from place to place, telling the good news. Philip went to the town of Samaria and told the people about Christ. They crowded around Philip because they were eager to hear what he was saying and to see him work miracles. Many people with evil spirits were healed, and the spirits went out of them with a shout. A lot of crippled and lame people were also healed. Everyone in that city was very glad because of what was happening.

For some time a man named Simon had lived in the city of Samaria and had amazed the people. He practiced witchcraft and claimed to be somebody great. Everyone, rich and poor, crowded around him. They said, "This man is the power of God called 'The Great Power.'"

For a long time Simon had used witchcraft to amaze the people, and they kept crowding around him. But when they believed what Philip was saying about God's kingdom and about the name of Jesus Christ, they were all baptized. Even Simon believed and was baptized. He stayed close to Philip, because he marveled at all the miracles and wonders.

When the apostles in Jerusalem heard that some people in Samaria had accepted God's message, they sent Peter and John. When the two apostles arrived, they prayed that the people would be given the Holy Spirit. Before this, the Holy Spirit had not been given to anyone in Samaria though some of them had been baptized in the name of the Lord Jesus. Peter and John then placed their hands on everyone who had faith in the Lord, and they were given the Holy Spirit.

Simon noticed that the Spirit was given only when

the apostles placed their hands on the people. So he brought money and said to Peter and John, "Let me have this power too! Then anyone I place my hands on will also be given the Holy Spirit."

Peter said to him, "You and your money will both end up in hell if you think you can buy God's gift! You don't have any part in this, and God sees that your heart is not right. Get rid of these evil thoughts and ask God to forgive you. I can see that you are jealous and bound by your evil ways."

Simon said, "Please pray to the Lord, so that what you said won't happen to me."

After Peter and John had preached about the Lord, they returned to Jerusalem. On their way they told the good news in many villages of Samaria.

Philip and an Ethiopian Official
(Acts 8.26-40)

The Lord's angel said to Philip, "Go south* along the desert road that leads from Jerusalem to Gaza."* So Philip left.

An important Ethiopian official happened to be going along that road in his chariot. He was the chief treasurer for Candace, the Queen of Ethiopia. The official had gone to

Jerusalem to worship and was now on his way home. He was sitting in his chariot, reading the book of the prophet Isaiah.

The Spirit told Philip to catch up with the chariot. Philip ran up close and heard the man reading aloud from the book of Isaiah. Philip asked him, "Do you understand what you are reading?"

The official answered, "How can I understand unless someone helps me?" He then invited Philip to come up and sit beside him.

The man was reading the passage that said,

"He was led like a sheep
　　on its way to be killed.
He was silent as a lamb,
whose wool
　　is being cut off,

and he did not say
    a word.
He was treated like a nobody
and did not receive
    a fair trial.
How can he have children,
if his life
    is snatched away?"

The official said to Philip, "Tell me, was the prophet talking about himself or about someone else?" So Philip began at this place in the Scriptures and explained the good news about Jesus.

As they were going along the road, they came to a place where there was some water. The official said, "Look! Here is some water. Why can't I be baptized?"* He ordered the chariot to stop. Then they both went down into the water, and Philip baptized him.

After they had come out of the water, the Lord's Spirit took Philip away. The official never saw him again, but he was very happy as he went on his way.

Philip later appeared in Azotus. He went from town to town, all the way to Caesarea, telling people about Jesus.

Saul Becomes a Follower of the Lord
(Acts 9.1-19)

Saul kept on threatening to kill the Lord's followers. He even went to the high priest and asked for letters to the Jewish leaders in Damascus. He did this because he wanted to arrest and take to Jerusalem any man or woman

who had accepted the Lord's Way.* When Saul had almost reached Damascus, a bright light from heaven suddenly flashed around him. He fell to the ground and heard a voice that said, "Saul! Saul! Why are you so cruel to me?"

"Who are you?" Saul asked.

"I am Jesus," the Lord answered. "I am the one you are so cruel to. Now get up and go into the city, where you will be told what to do."

The men with Saul stood there speechless. They had heard the voice, but they had not seen anyone. Saul got up from the ground, and when he opened his eyes, he could not see a thing. Someone then led him by the hand to Damascus, and for three days he was blind and did not eat or drink.

A follower named Ananias lived in Damascus, and the Lord spoke to him in a vision. Ananias answered, "Lord, here I am."

The Lord said to him, "Get up and go to the house of Judas on Straight Street. When you get there, you will find a man named Saul from the city of Tarsus. Saul is praying, and he has seen a vision. He saw a man named Ananias coming to him and putting his hands on him, so that he could see again."

Ananias replied, "Lord, a lot of people have told me about the terrible things this man has done to your followers in Jerusalem. Now the chief priests have given him the power to come here and arrest anyone who worships in your name."

The Lord said to Ananias, "Go! I have chosen him to tell foreigners, kings, and the people of Israel about me. I will show him how much he must suffer for worshiping in my name."

Ananias left and went into the house where Saul was

staying. Ananias placed his hands on him and said, "Saul, the Lord Jesus has sent me. He is the same one who appeared to you along the road. He wants you to be able to see and to be filled with the Holy Spirit."

Suddenly something like fish scales fell from Saul's eyes, and he could see. He got up and was baptized. Then he ate and felt much better.

Saul Preaches in Damascus
(Acts 9.19-25)

For several days Saul stayed with the Lord's followers in Damascus. Soon he went to the Jewish meeting places and started telling people that Jesus is the Son of God. Everyone who heard Saul was amazed and said, "Isn't this the man who caused so much trouble for those people in Jerusalem who worship in the name of Jesus? Didn't he come here to arrest them and take them to the chief priests?"

Saul preached with such power that he completely confused the Jewish people in Damascus, as he tried to show them that Jesus is the Messiah.

Later some of them made plans to kill Saul, but he found out about it. He learned that they were guarding the gates of the city day and night in order to kill him. Then one night his followers let him down over the city wall in a large basket.

Saul in Jerusalem
(Acts 9.26-31)

When Saul arrived in Jerusalem, he tried to join the followers. But they were all afraid of him, because they did not believe he was a true follower. Then Barnabas helped him by taking him to the apostles. He explained how on the road to Damascus, Saul had seen the Lord and how the Lord had spoken to Saul. Barnabas also said that when Saul was in Damascus, he had spoken bravely in the name of Jesus.

Saul moved about freely with the followers in Jerusalem and told everyone about the Lord. He was always arguing with the Jews who spoke Greek, and so they tried to kill him. But the followers found out about this and took Saul to Caesarea. From there they sent him to the city of Tarsus.

The church in Judea, Galilee, and Samaria now had a time of peace and kept on worshiping the Lord. The church became stronger, as the Holy Spirit encouraged it and helped it grow.

Peter Heals Aeneas
(Acts 9.32-35)

While Peter was traveling from place to place, he visited the Lord's followers who lived in the town of Lydda.

There he met a man named Aeneas, who for eight years had been sick in bed and could not move. Peter said to Aeneas, "Jesus Christ has healed you! Get up and make up your bed."* Right away he stood up.

Many people in the towns of Lydda and Sharon saw Aeneas and became followers of the Lord.

Peter Brings Dorcas Back to Life
(Acts 9.36-43)

In Joppa there was a follower named Tabitha. Her Greek name was Dorcas, which means "deer." She was always doing good things for people and had given much to the poor. But she got sick and died, and her body was washed and placed in an upstairs room. Joppa was not far from Lydda, and the followers heard that Peter was there. They sent two men to say to him, "Please come with us as quickly as you can!" Right away Peter went with them.

The men took Peter upstairs into the room. Many widows were there crying. They showed him the coats and clothes that Dorcas had made while she was still alive.

After Peter had sent everyone out of the room, he kneeled down and prayed. Then he turned to the body of Dorcas and said, "Tabitha, get up!" The woman opened her eyes, and when she saw Peter, she sat up. He took her by the hand and helped her to her feet.

Peter called in the widows and the other followers and showed them that Dorcas had been raised from death. Everyone in Joppa heard what had happened, and many of them put their faith in the Lord. Peter stayed on for a while in Joppa in the house of a man named Simon, who made leather.

Peter and Cornelius
(Acts 10.1-48)

In Caesarea there was a man named Cornelius, who was the captain of a group of soldiers called "The Italian Unit." Cornelius was a very religious man. He worshiped God, and so did everyone else who lived in his house. He had given a lot of money to the poor and was always praying to God.

One afternoon at about three o'clock,* Cornelius had a vision. He saw an angel from God coming to him and calling him by name. Cornelius was surprised and stared at the angel. Then he asked, "What is this all about?"

The angel answered, "God has heard your prayers and knows about your gifts to the poor. Now send some men to Joppa for a man named Simon Peter. He is visiting with Simon the leather maker, who lives in a house near the sea." After saying this, the angel left.

Cornelius called in two of his servants and one of his

soldiers who worshiped God. He explained everything to them and sent them off to Joppa.

The next day about noon these men were coming near to Joppa. Peter went up on the roof* of the house to pray and became very hungry. While the food was being prepared, he fell sound asleep and had a vision. He saw heaven open, and something came down like a huge sheet held up by its four corners. In it were all kinds of animals, snakes, and birds. A voice said to him, "Peter, get up! Kill these and eat them."

But Peter said, "Lord, I can't do that! I've never eaten anything that is unclean and not fit to eat."*

The voice spoke to him again, "When God says that something can be used for food, don't say it isn't fit to eat."

This happened three times before the sheet was suddenly taken back to heaven.

Peter was still wondering what all of this meant, when the men sent by Cornelius came and stood at the gate. They had found their way to Simon's house and were asking if Simon Peter was staying there.

While Peter was still thinking about the vision, the Holy Spirit said to him, "Three* men are here looking for you. Hurry down and go with them. Don't worry, I sent them."

Peter went down and said to the men, "I am the one you are looking for. Why have you come?"

They answered, "Captain Cornelius sent us. He is a good man and worships God. All the Jewish people like him. One of God's holy angels told Cornelius to send for you, so he could hear what you have to say." Peter invited them to spend the night.

The next morning Peter and some of the Lord's followers in Joppa left with the men who had come from

Cornelius. The next day they all arrived in Caesarea where Cornelius was waiting for them. He had also invited his relatives and close friends.

When Peter arrived, Cornelius greeted him. Then he kneeled at Peter's feet and started worshiping him. But Peter took hold of him and said, "Stand up! I am nothing more than a human."

As Peter entered the house, he was still talking with Cornelius. Many people were there, and Peter said to them, "You know that we Jews are not allowed to have anything to do with other people. But God has shown me that he doesn't think anyone is unclean or unfit. I agreed to come here, but I want to know why you sent for me."

Cornelius answered:

Four days ago at about three o'clock in the afternoon I was praying at home. Suddenly a man in bright clothes stood in front of me. He said, "Cornelius, God has heard your prayers, and he knows about your gifts to the poor. Now send to Joppa for Simon Peter. He is visiting in the home of Simon the leather maker, who lives near the sea."

I sent for you right away, and you have been good enough to come. All of us are here in the presence of the Lord God, so that we can hear what he has to say.

Peter then said:

Now I am certain that God treats all people alike. God is pleased with everyone who worships

him and does right, no matter what nation they come from. This is the same message that God gave to the people of Israel, when he sent Jesus Christ, the Lord of all, to offer peace to them.

You surely know what happened* everywhere in Judea. It all began in Galilee after John had told everyone to be baptized. God gave the Holy Spirit and power to Jesus from Nazareth. He was with Jesus, as he went around doing good and healing everyone who was under the power of the devil. We all saw what Jesus did both in Israel and in the city of Jerusalem.

Jesus was put to death on a cross. But three days later, God raised him to life and let him be seen. Not everyone saw him. He was seen only by us, who ate and drank with him after he was raised from death. We were the ones God chose to tell others about him.

God told us to announce clearly to the people that Jesus is the one he has chosen to judge the living and the dead. Every one of the prophets has said that all who have faith in Jesus will have their sins forgiven in his name.

While Peter was still speaking, the Holy Spirit took control of everyone who was listening. Some Jewish followers of the Lord had come with Peter, and they were surprised that the Holy Spirit had been given to Gentiles. Now they were hearing Gentiles speaking unknown languages and praising God.

Peter said, "These Gentiles have been given the Holy Spirit, just as we have! I am certain that no one would dare stop us from baptizing them." Peter ordered them to be baptized in the name of Jesus Christ, and they asked him to stay on for a few days.

Peter Reports to the Church
in Jerusalem

(Acts 11.1-18)

The apostles and the followers in Judea heard that Gentiles had accepted God's message. So when Peter came to Jerusalem, some of the Jewish leaders started arguing with him. They wanted Gentile followers to be circumcised, and they said, "You stayed in the homes of Gentiles, and you even ate with them!"

Then Peter told them exactly what had happened:

I was in the town of Joppa and was praying when I fell sound asleep and had a vision. I saw heaven open, and something like a huge sheet held by its four corners came down to me. When I looked in it, I saw animals, wild beasts, snakes, and birds. I heard a voice saying to me, "Peter, get up! Kill these and eat them."

But I said, "Lord, I can't do that! I've never taken a bite of anything that is unclean and not fit to eat."*

The voice from heaven spoke to me again, "When God says that something can be used for food, don't say it isn't fit to eat." This happened three times before it was all taken back into heaven.

Suddenly three men from Caesarea stood in front of the house where I was staying. The Holy Spirit told me to go with them and not to worry. Then six of the Lord's followers went with me to the home of a man who told us that an angel had appeared to him. The angel had ordered him to send to Joppa for someone named Simon Peter. Then Peter would tell him how he and everyone in his house could be saved.

After I started speaking, the Holy Spirit was given to them, just as the Spirit had been given to us at the beginning. I remembered that the Lord had said, "John baptized with water, but you will be baptized with the Holy Spirit." God gave those Gentiles the same gift that he gave us when we put our faith in the Lord Jesus Christ. So how could I have gone against God?

When the Jewish leaders heard Peter say this, they stopped arguing and started praising God. They said, "God has now let Gentiles turn to him, and he has given life to them!"

The Church in Antioch
(Acts 11.19-30)

Some of the Lord's followers had been scattered because of the terrible trouble that started when Stephen was killed. They went as far as Phoenicia, Cyprus, and Antioch, but they told the message only to the Jews.

Some of the followers from Cyprus and Cyrene went to Antioch and started telling Gentiles* the good news about the Lord Jesus. The Lord's power was with them, and many people turned to the Lord and put their faith in him. News of what was happening reached the church in Jerusalem. Then they sent Barnabas to Antioch.

When Barnabas got there and saw what God had been kind enough to do for them, he was very glad. So he begged them to remain faithful to the Lord with all their hearts. Barnabas was a good man of great faith, and he was

filled with the Holy Spirit. Many more people turned to the Lord.

Barnabas went to Tarsus to look for Saul. He found Saul and brought him to Antioch, where they met with the church for a whole year and taught many of its people. There in Antioch the Lord's followers were first called Christians.

During this time some prophets from Jerusalem came to Antioch. One of them was Agabus. Then with the help of the Spirit, he told that there would be a terrible famine everywhere in the world. And it happened when Claudius was Emperor.* The followers in Antioch decided to send whatever help they could to the followers in Judea. So they had Barnabas and Saul take their gifts to the church leaders in Jerusalem.

Herod Causes Trouble for the Church
(Acts 12.1-5)

At that time King Herod* caused terrible suffering for some members of the church. He ordered soldiers to cut off the head of James, the brother of John. When Herod saw that this pleased the Jewish people, he had Peter arrested during the Feast of Thin Bread. He put Peter in jail and ordered four squads of soldiers to guard him. Herod planned to put him on trial in public after the feast.

While Peter was being kept in jail, the church never stopped praying to God for him.

Peter Is Rescued
(Acts 12.6-19)

The night before Peter was to be put on trial, he was asleep and bound by two chains. A soldier was guarding him on each side, and two other soldiers were guarding the entrance to the jail. Suddenly an angel from the Lord appeared, and light flashed around in the cell. The angel poked Peter in the side and woke him up. Then he said, "Quick! Get up!"

The chains fell off his hands, and the angel said, "Get dressed and put on your sandals." Peter did what he was told. Then the angel said, "Now put on your coat and follow me." Peter left with the angel, but he thought everything was only a dream. They went past the two groups of soldiers, and when they came to the iron gate to the city, it opened by itself. They went out and were going along the street, when all at once the angel disappeared.

Peter now realized what had happened, and he said, "I am certain that the Lord sent his angel to rescue me from Herod and from everything the Jewish leaders planned to do to me." Then Peter went to the house of Mary the mother

of John whose other name was Mark. Many of the Lord's followers had come together there and were praying.

Peter knocked on the gate, and a servant named Rhoda came to the door. When she heard Peter's voice, she was too excited to open the gate. She ran back into the house and said that Peter was standing there.

Everyone told her, "You are crazy!" But she kept saying that it was Peter. Then they said, "It must be his angel."* But Peter kept on knocking, until finally they opened the gate. They saw him and were completely amazed.

Peter motioned for them to keep quiet. Then he told how the Lord had led him out of jail. He also said, "Tell James and the others what has happened." After that, he left and went somewhere else.

The next morning the soldiers who had been on guard were terribly worried and wondered what had happened to Peter. Herod ordered his own soldiers to search for him, but they could not find him. Then he questioned the guards and had them put to death. After this, Herod left Judea to stay in Caesarea for a while.

Herod Dies

(Acts 12.20-25)

Herod and the people of Tyre and Sidon were very angry with each other. But their country got its food supply from the region that he ruled. So a group of them went to see Blastus, who was one of Herod's high officials. They convinced Blastus that they wanted to make peace between their cities and Herod, and a day was set for them to meet with him.

Herod came dressed in his royal robes. He sat down on his throne and made a speech. The people shouted, "You speak more like a god than a man!" At once an angel from the Lord struck him down because he took the honor that belonged to God. Later, Herod was eaten by worms and died.

God's message kept spreading. And after Barnabas

and Saul had done the work they were sent to do, they went back to Jerusalem* with John, whose other name was Mark.

Barnabas and Saul Are Chosen and Sent
(Acts 13.1-3)

The church at Antioch had several prophets and teachers. They were Barnabas, Simeon, also called Niger, Lucius from Cyrene, Manaen, who was Herod's* close friend, and Saul. While they were worshiping the Lord and going without eating,* the Holy Spirit told them, "Appoint Barnabas and Saul to do the work for which I have chosen them." Everyone prayed and went without eating for a while longer. Next, they placed their hands on Barnabas and Saul to show that they had been appointed to do this work. Then everyone sent them on their way.

Barnabas and Saul in Cyprus
(Acts 13.4-12)

After Barnabas and Saul had been sent by the Holy Spirit, they went to Seleucia. From there they sailed to the island of Cyprus. They arrived at Salamis and began to preach God's message in the Jewish meeting places. They also had John* as a helper.

They went all the way to the city of Paphos on the other end of the island, where they met a Jewish man named Bar-Jesus. He practiced witchcraft and was a false prophet. He also worked for Sergius Paulus, who was very smart and was the governor of the island. Sergius Paulus wanted to hear God's message, and he sent for Barnabas and Saul. But Bar-Jesus, whose other name was Elymas, was against them. He even tried to keep the governor from having faith in the Lord.

Then Saul, better known as Paul, was filled with the Holy Spirit. He looked straight at Elymas and said, "You son of the devil! You are a liar, a crook, and an enemy of everything that is right. When will you stop speaking against the true ways of the Lord? The Lord is going to punish you by making you completely blind for a while."

Suddenly the man's eyes were covered by a dark mist, and he went around trying to get someone to lead him by the hand. When the governor saw what had happened, he was amazed at this teaching about the Lord. So he put his faith in the Lord.

Paul and Barnabas in Antioch of Pisidia
(Acts 13.13-52)

Paul and the others left Paphos and sailed to Perga in Pamphylia. But John* left them and went back to

Jerusalem. The rest of them went on from Perga to Antioch in Pisidia. Then on the Sabbath they went to the Jewish meeting place and sat down.

After the reading of the Law and the Prophets,* the leaders sent someone over to tell Paul and Barnabas, "Friends, if you have anything to say that will help the people, please say it."

Paul got up. He motioned with his hand and said:

People of Israel, and everyone else who worships God, listen! The God of Israel chose our ancestors, and he let our people prosper while they were living in Egypt. Then with his mighty power he led them out, and for about forty years he took care of* them in the desert. He destroyed seven nations in the land of Canaan and gave their land to our people. All this happened in about 450 years.

Then God gave our people judges until the time of the prophet Samuel, but the people demanded a king. So for forty years God gave them King Saul, the son of Kish from the tribe of Benjamin. Later, God removed Saul and let David rule in his place. God said about him, "David the son of Jesse is the kind of person who pleases me most! He does everything I want him to do."

God promised that someone from David's family would come to save the people of Israel, and Jesus is that one. But before Jesus came, John was telling everyone in Israel to turn back to God and be baptized. Then, when John's work was almost done, he said, "Who do you people think I am? Do you think I am the Promised One? He will come later, and I am not good enough to untie his sandals."

Now listen, you descendants of Abraham! Pay attention, all of you Gentiles who are here to worship God! Listen to this message about how to be saved, because it is for everyone. The people of Jerusalem and their leaders didn't realize who Jesus was. And they didn't understand the words of the prophets that they read each Sabbath. So they condemned Jesus just as the prophets had said.

They did exactly what the Scriptures said they would. Even though they couldn't find any reason to put Jesus to death, they still asked Pilate to have him killed.

After Jesus had been put to death, he was taken down from the cross* and put in a tomb. But God raised him from death! Then for many days Jesus appeared to his followers who had gone with him from Galilee to Jerusalem. Now they are telling our people about him.

God made a promise to our ancestors. And we are here to tell you the good news that he has kept this promise to us. It is just as the second Psalm says about Jesus,

"You are my son because today
        I have become your Father."

God raised Jesus from death and will never let his body decay. It is just as God said,

"I will make to you
    the same holy promise
        that I made to David."

And in another psalm it says, "God will never let the body of his Holy One decay."

When David was alive, he obeyed God. Then after he died, he was buried in the family grave, and his body decayed. But God raised Jesus from death, and his body did not decay.

My friends, the message is that Jesus can forgive your sins! The Law of Moses could not set you free from all your sins. But everyone who has faith in Jesus is set free. Make sure that what the prophets have said doesn't happen to you. They said,

> "Look, you people
>> who make fun of God!
> Be amazed
>> and disappear.
> I will do something today
>> that you won't believe,
> even if someone
>> tells you about it!"

As Paul and Barnabas were leaving the meeting, the people begged them to say more about these same things on the next Sabbath. After the service, many Jews and a lot of Gentiles who worshiped God went with them. Paul and Barnabas begged them all to remain faithful to God, who had been so kind to them.

The next Sabbath almost everyone in town came to hear the message about the Lord.* When the Jewish people saw the crowds, they were very jealous. They insulted Paul and spoke against everything he said.

But Paul and Barnabas bravely said:

> We had to tell God's message to you before we told it to anyone else. But you rejected the message! This proves that you don't deserve eternal life. Now

we are going to the Gentiles. The Lord has given us this command,

> "I have placed you here
>> as a light
>>> for the Gentiles.
> You are to take
>> the saving power of God
> to people everywhere
>> on earth."

This message made the Gentiles glad, and they praised what they had heard about the Lord.* Everyone who had been chosen for eternal life then put their faith in the Lord.

The message about the Lord spread all over that region. But the Jewish leaders went to some of the important men in the town and to some respected women who were religious. They turned them against Paul and Barnabas and started making trouble for them. They even chased them out of that part of the country.

Paul and Barnabas shook the dust from that place off their feet* and went on to the city of Iconium.

But the Lord's followers in Antioch were very happy and were filled with the Holy Spirit.

Paul and Barnabas in Iconium
(Acts 14.1-7)

Paul and Barnabas spoke in the Jewish meeting place in Iconium, just as they had done at Antioch, and many Jews and Gentiles* put their faith in the Lord. But

the Jews who did not have faith in him made the other Gentiles angry and turned them against the Lord's followers.

Paul and Barnabas stayed there for a while, having faith in the Lord and bravely speaking his message. The Lord gave them the power to work miracles and wonders, and he showed that their message about his great kindness was true.

The people of Iconium did not know what to think. Some of them believed the Jewish group, and others believed the apostles. Finally, some Gentiles and Jews, together with their leaders, decided to make trouble for Paul and Barnabas and to kill them by throwing stones at them.

But when the two apostles found out what was happening, they escaped to the region of Lycaonia. They preached the good news there in the towns of Lystra and Derbe and in the nearby countryside.

Paul and Barnabas in Lystra
(Acts 14.8-20)

In Lystra there was a man who had been born with crippled feet and had never been able to walk. The man was listening to Paul speak, when Paul saw that he had faith in Jesus and could be healed. So he looked straight at the man and shouted, "Stand up!" The man jumped up and started walking around.

When the crowd saw what Paul had done, they yelled out in the language of Lycaonia, "The gods have turned into humans and have come down to us!" They gave Barnabas the name Zeus, and they gave Paul the name Hermes,* because he did the talking.

The temple of Zeus was near the entrance to the city.

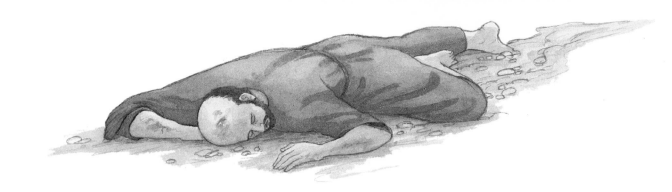

Its priest and the crowds wanted to offer a sacrifice to Barnabas and Paul. So the priest brought some bulls and flowers to the city gates. When the two apostles found out about this, they tore their clothes in horror and ran to the crowd, shouting:

Why are you doing this? We are humans just like you. Please give up all this foolishness. Turn to the living God, who made the sky, the earth, the sea, and everything in them. In times past, God let each nation go its own way. But he showed that he was there by the good things he did. God sends rain from heaven and makes your crops grow. He gives food to you and makes your hearts glad.

Even after Paul and Barnabas had said all this, they could hardly keep the people from offering a sacrifice to them.

Some Jewish leaders from Antioch and Iconium came and turned the crowds against Paul. They hit him with stones and dragged him out of the city, thinking he was dead. But when the Lord's followers gathered around Paul, he stood up and went back into the city. The next day he and Barnabas went to Derbe.

Paul and Barnabas Return to Antioch in Syria

(Acts 14.21—15.2)

Paul and Barnabas preached the good news in Derbe and won some people to the Lord. Then they went back to

Lystra, Iconium, and Antioch in Pisidia. They encouraged the followers and begged them to remain faithful. They told them, "We have to suffer a lot before we can get into God's kingdom." Paul and Barnabas chose some of those who had faith in the Lord to be leaders for each of the churches. Then they went without eating* and prayed that the Lord would take good care of these leaders.

Paul and Barnabas went on through Pisidia to Pamphylia, where they preached in the town of Perga. Then they went down to Attalia and sailed to Antioch in Syria. It was there that they had been placed in God's care for the work they had now completed.*

After arriving in Antioch, they called the church together. They told the people what God had helped them do and how he had made it possible for the Gentiles to believe. Then they stayed there with the followers for a long time.

Some people came from Judea and started teaching the Lord's followers that they could not be saved, unless they were circumcised as Moses had taught. This caused trouble, and Paul and Barnabas argued with them about this teaching. So it was decided to send Paul and Barnabas and a few others to Jerusalem to discuss this problem with the apostles and the church leaders.

The Church Leaders Meet in Jerusalem
(Acts 15.3-21)

The men who were sent by the church went through Phoenicia and Samaria and told how the Gentiles had turned to God. This news made the Lord's followers very happy. When the men arrived in Jerusalem, they were welcomed by all the church, including the apostles and the leaders. They told them everything that God had helped them do. But some Pharisees had become followers of the Lord. They stood up and said, "Gentiles who have faith in the Lord must be circumcised and told to obey the Law of Moses."

The apostles and church leaders met to discuss this problem about Gentiles. They had talked it over for a long time, when Peter got up and said:

My friends, you know that God decided long ago to let me be the one from your group to preach the good news to the Gentiles. God did this so that they would hear and obey him. He knows what is in everyone's heart. And he showed that he had chosen the Gentiles, when he gave them the Holy Spirit, just as he had given his Spirit to us. God treated them in the same way that he treated us. They put their faith in him, and he made their hearts pure.

Now why are you trying to make God angry by placing a heavy burden on these followers? This burden was too heavy for us or our ancestors. But our Lord Jesus was kind to us Jews, and we are saved by faith in him, just as the Gentiles are.

Everyone kept quiet and listened as Barnabas and Paul told how God had given them the power to work a lot of miracles and wonders for the Gentiles.

After they had finished speaking, James* said:

My friends, listen to me! Simon Peter* has told how God first came to the Gentiles and made some of them his own people. This agrees with what the prophets wrote,

"I, the Lord, will return
and rebuild
David's fallen house.

I will build it from its ruins
	and set it up again.
Then other nations
will turn to me
	and be my chosen ones.
I, the Lord, say this.
		I promised it long ago."

And so, my friends, I don't think we should place burdens on the Gentiles who are turning to God. We should simply write and tell them not to eat anything that has been offered to idols. They should be told not to eat the meat of any animal that has been strangled or that still has blood in it. They must also not commit any terrible sexual sins.*

We must remember that the Law of Moses has been preached in city after city for many years, and every Sabbath it is read when we Jews meet.

A Letter to Gentiles Who Had Faith in the Lord

(Acts 15.22-35)

The apostles, the leaders, and all the church members decided to send some men to Antioch along with Paul and Barnabas. They chose Silas and Judas Barsabbas,* who were two leaders of the Lord's followers. They wrote a letter that said:

> We apostles and leaders send friendly greetings to all of you Gentiles who are followers of the Lord in Antioch, Syria, and Cilicia.
>
> We have heard that some people from here have terribly upset you by what they said. But we did not send them! So we met together and decided to choose some men and to send them to you along with our good friends Barnabas and Paul. These men have risked their lives for our Lord Jesus Christ. We are also sending Judas and Silas, who will tell you in person the same things that we are writing.
>
> The Holy Spirit has shown us that we should not place any extra burden on you. But you should not eat anything offered to idols. You should not eat any meat that still has the blood in it or any meat of any animal that has been strangled. You must also not commit any terrible sexual sins. If you follow these instructions, you will do well.
>
> We send our best wishes.

The four men left Jerusalem and went to Antioch. Then they called all the church members together and gave them the letter. When the letter was read, it made everyone glad and gave them lots of encouragement. Judas and Silas were prophets, and they spoke a long time, encouraging and helping the Lord's followers.

The men from Jerusalem stayed on in Antioch for a while. And when they left to return to the ones who had sent them, the followers wished them well. But Silas, Paul, and Barnabas stayed on in Antioch, where they and many others taught and preached about the Lord.*

Paul and Barnabas Go Their Separate Ways
(Acts 15.36-41)

Sometime later Paul said to Barnabas, "Let's go back and visit the Lord's followers in all the cities where we preached his message. Then we will know how they are doing." Barnabas wanted to take along John, whose other name was Mark. But Paul did not want to, because Mark had left them in Pamphylia and had stopped working with them.

Paul and Barnabas argued, then each of them went his own way. Barnabas took Mark and sailed to Cyprus, but Paul took Silas and left after the followers had placed them in God's care. They traveled through Syria and Cilicia, encouraging the churches.

Timothy Works with Paul and Silas
(Acts 16.1-5)

Paul and Silas went back to Derbe and Lystra, where there was a follower named Timothy. His mother was also a follower. She was Jewish, and his father was Greek. The Lord's followers in Lystra and Iconium said good things about Timothy, and Paul wanted him to go with them. But Paul first had him circumcised, because all the Jewish people around there knew that Timothy's father was Greek.*

As Paul and the others went from city to city, they

told the followers what the apostles and leaders in Jerusalem had decided, and they urged them to follow these instructions. The churches became stronger in their faith, and each day more people put their faith in the Lord.

Paul's Vision in Troas
(Acts 16.6-10)

Paul and his friends went through Phrygia and Galatia, but the Holy Spirit would not let them preach in Asia. After they arrived in Mysia, they tried to go into Bithynia, but the Spirit of Jesus would not let them. So they went on through Mysia until they came to Troas.

During the night, Paul had a vision of someone from Macedonia who was standing there and begging him, "Come over to Macedonia and help us!" After Paul had seen the vision, we began looking for a way to go to Macedonia. We were sure that God had called us to preach the good news there.

Lydia Becomes a Follower of the Lord
(Acts 16.11-15)

We sailed from Troas and went straight to Samothrace. The next day we arrived in Neapolis. From there we went to Philippi, which is a Roman colony in the first district of Macedonia.*

We spent several days in Philippi. Then on the Sabbath we went outside the city gate to a place by the river, where we thought there would be a Jewish meeting place for prayer. We sat down and talked with the women who came. One of them was Lydia, who was from the city of Thyatira and sold expensive purple cloth. She was a worshiper of the Lord God, and he made her willing to accept what Paul was saying. Then after she and her family

were baptized, she kept on begging us, "If you think I really do have faith in the Lord, come stay in my home." Finally, we accepted her invitation.

Paul and Silas Are Put in Jail
(Acts 16.16-40)

One day on our way to the place of prayer, we were met by a slave girl. She had a spirit in her that gave her the power to tell the future. By doing this she made a lot of money for her owners. The girl followed Paul and the rest of us and kept yelling, "These men are servants of the Most High God! They are telling you how to be saved."

This went on for several days. Finally, Paul got so upset that he turned and said to the spirit, "In the name of Jesus Christ, I order you to leave this girl alone!" At once the evil spirit left her.

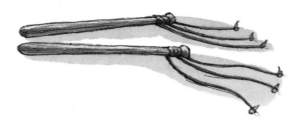

When the girl's owners realized that they had lost all chances for making more money, they grabbed Paul and Silas and dragged them into court. They told the officials, "These Jews are upsetting our city! They are telling us to do things we Romans are not allowed to do."

The crowd joined in the attack on Paul and Silas. Then the officials tore the clothes off the two men and ordered them to be beaten with a whip. After they had been badly beaten, they were put in jail, and the jailer was told to guard them carefully. The jailer did as he was told. He put them deep inside the jail and chained their feet to heavy blocks of wood.

About midnight Paul and Silas were praying and singing praises to God, while the other prisoners listened. Suddenly a strong earthquake shook the jail to its foundations. The doors opened, and the chains fell from all the prisoners.

When the jailer woke up and saw that the doors were open, he thought that the prisoners had escaped. He pulled out his sword and was about to kill himself. But Paul shouted, "Don't harm yourself! No one has escaped."

The jailer asked for a torch and went into the jail. He was shaking all over as he kneeled down in front of Paul and Silas. After he had led them out of the jail, he asked, "What must I do to be saved?"

They replied, "Have faith in the Lord Jesus and you will be saved! This is also true for everyone who lives in your home."

Then Paul and Silas told him and everyone else in his house about the Lord. While it was still night, the jailer took them to a place where he could wash their cuts and bruises. Then he and everyone in his home were baptized. They were very glad that they had put their faith in God. After this, the jailer took Paul and Silas to his home and gave them something to eat.

The next morning the officials sent some police with orders for the jailer to let Paul and Silas go. The jailer told Paul, "The officials have ordered me to set you free. Now you can leave in peace."

But Paul told the police, "We are Roman citizens,* and the Roman officials had us beaten in public without giving us a trial. They threw us into jail. Now do they think they can secretly send us away? No, they cannot! They will have to come here themselves and let us out."

When the police told the officials that Paul and Silas were Roman citizens, the officials were afraid. So they came and apologized. They led them out of the jail and asked them to please leave town. But Paul and Silas went straight to the home of Lydia, where they saw the Lord's followers and encouraged them. Then they left.

Trouble in Thessalonica
(Acts 17.1-9)

After Paul and his friends had traveled through Amphipolis and Apollonia, they went on to Thessalonica. A Jewish meeting place was in that city. So as usual, Paul went there to worship, and on three Sabbaths he spoke to the people. He used the Scriptures to show them that the Messiah had to suffer, but that he would rise from death. Paul also told them that Jesus is the Messiah he was preaching about. Some of the Jews believed what Paul had said, and they became followers with Paul and Silas. Some Gentiles* and many important women also believed the message.

The Jewish leaders were jealous and got some worthless bums who hung around the marketplace to start a riot in the city. They wanted to drag Paul and Silas out to the mob, and so they went straight to Jason's home. But when they did not find them there, they dragged out Jason and some of the Lord's followers. They took them to the city authorities and shouted, "Paul and Silas have been upsetting things everywhere. Now they have come here, and Jason has welcomed them into his home. All of them break the laws of the Roman Emperor by claiming that someone named Jesus is king."

The officials and all the people were upset when they heard this. So they made Jason and the other followers pay bail before they would let them go.

People in Berea Welcome the Message
(Acts 17.10-15)

That same night the Lord's followers sent Paul and Silas on to Berea, and after they arrived, they went to the Jewish meeting place. The people in Berea were much nicer than those in Thessalonica, and they gladly accepted the message. Day after day they studied the Scriptures to see if these things were true. Many of them put their faith in the Lord, including some important Greek women and several men.

When the Jewish leaders in Thessalonica heard that Paul had been preaching God's message in Berea, they went there and caused trouble by turning the crowds against Paul.

Right away the followers sent Paul down to the coast,

but Silas and Timothy stayed in Thessalonica. Some men went with Paul as far as Athens. They returned with instructions for Silas and Timothy to join him as soon as possible.

Paul in Athens
(Acts 17.16-34)

While Paul was waiting in Athens, he was upset to see all the idols in the city. He went to the Jewish meeting place to speak to the Jews and to anyone who worshiped with them. Day after day he also spoke to everyone he met in the market. Some of them were Epicureans* and some were Stoics,* and they started arguing with him.

People were asking, "What is this know-it-all trying to say?"

Some even said, "Paul must be preaching about foreign gods! That's what he means when he talks about Jesus and about people rising from death."*

They brought Paul before a council called the Areopagus, and said, "Tell us what your new teaching is all about. We have heard you say some strange things, and we want to know what it means."

More than anything else the people of Athens and the foreigners living there loved to hear and to talk about anything new. So Paul stood up in front of the council and said:

People of Athens, I see that you are very religious. As I was going through your city and looking at the things you worship, I found an altar with the words, "To an Unknown God." You worship

this God, but you don't really know him. So I want to tell you about him. This God made the world and everything in it. He is Lord of heaven and earth, and he doesn't live in temples built by human hands. He doesn't need help from anyone. He gives life, breath, and everything else to all people. From one person God made all nations who live on earth, and he decided when and where every nation would be.

God has done all this, so that we will look for him and reach out and find him. He is not far from any of us, and he gives us the power to live, to move, and to be who we are. "We are his children," just as some of your poets have said.

Since we are God's children, we must not think that he is like an idol made out of gold or silver or stone. He is not like anything that humans have thought up and made. In the past God forgave all this because people did not know what they were doing. But now he says that everyone everywhere must turn to him. He has set a day when he will judge all the world's people with fairness. And he has chosen the man Jesus to do the judging for him. God has given proof of this to all of us by raising Jesus from death.

As soon as the people heard Paul say that a man had been raised from death, some of them started laughing. Others said, "We'll hear you talk about this some other time." When Paul left the council meeting, some of the men put their faith in the Lord and went with Paul. One of them was a council member named Dionysius. A woman named Damaris and several others also put their faith in the Lord.

Paul in Corinth

(Acts 18.1-17)

Paul left Athens and went to Corinth, where he met Aquila, a Jewish man from Pontus. Not long before this, Aquila had come from Italy with his wife Priscilla, because Emperor Claudius had ordered all the Jewish people to leave Rome.* Paul went to see Aquila and Priscilla and found out that they were tent makers. Paul was a tent maker too. So he stayed with them, and they worked together.

Every Sabbath Paul went to the Jewish meeting

place. He spoke to Jews and Gentiles* and tried to win them over. But after Silas and Timothy came from Macedonia, he spent all his time preaching to the Jews about Jesus the Messiah. Finally, they turned against him and insulted him. So he shook the dust from his clothes* and told them, "Whatever happens to you will be your own fault! I am not to blame. From now on I am going to preach to the Gentiles."

Paul then moved into the house of a man named Titius Justus, who worshiped God and lived next door to the Jewish meeting place. Crispus was the leader of the meeting place. He and everyone in his family put their faith in the Lord. Many others in Corinth also heard the message, and all the people who had faith in the Lord were baptized.

One night Paul had a vision, and in it the Lord said, "Don't be afraid to keep on preaching. Don't stop! I am with you, and you won't be harmed. Many people in this city belong to me." Paul stayed on in Corinth for a year and a half, teaching God's message to the people.

While Gallio was governor of Achaia, some of the Jewish leaders got together and grabbed Paul. They brought him into court and said, "This man is trying to make our people worship God in a way that is against our Law!"

Even before Paul could speak, Gallio said, "If you were charging this man with a crime or some other wrong, I would have to listen to you. But since this concerns only words, names, and your own law, you will have to take care of it. I refuse to judge such matters." Then he sent them all out of the court. The crowd grabbed Sosthenes, the Jewish leader, and beat him up in front of the court. But none of this mattered to Gallio.

Paul Returns to Antioch in Syria
(Acts 18.18-23)

After Paul had stayed for a while with the Lord's followers in Corinth, he told them good-by and sailed on to Syria with Aquila and Priscilla. But before he left, he had his head shaved* at Cenchreae because he had made a promise to God.

The three of them arrived in Ephesus, where Paul left Priscilla and Aquila. He then went into the Jewish meeting place to talk with the people there. They asked him to stay longer, but he refused. He told them good-by and said, "If God lets me, I will come back."

Paul sailed to Caesarea, where he greeted the church. Then he went on to Antioch. After staying there for a while, he left and visited several places in Galatia and Phrygia. He helped all the followers there to become stronger in their faith.

Apollos in Ephesus
(Acts 18.24-28)

A Jewish man named Apollos came to Ephesus. Apollos had been born in the city of Alexandria. He was a very good speaker and knew a lot about the Scriptures. He also knew much about the Lord's Way,* and he spoke about it with great excitement. What he taught about Jesus was right, but all he knew was John's message about baptism.

Apollos started speaking bravely in the Jewish meeting place. But when Priscilla and Aquila heard him, they took him to their home and helped him understand God's Way even better.

Apollos decided to travel through Achaia. So the Lord's followers wrote letters and encouraged the followers there to welcome him. After Apollos arrived in Achaia, he

was a great help to everyone who had put their faith in the Lord Jesus because of God's kindness. He got into fierce arguments with the Jewish people, and in public he used the Scriptures to prove that Jesus is the Messiah.

Paul in Ephesus

(Acts 19.1-10)

While Apollos was in Corinth, Paul traveled across the hill country to Ephesus, where he met some of the Lord's followers. He asked them, "When you put your faith in Jesus, were you given the Holy Spirit?"

"No!" they answered. "We have never even heard of the Holy Spirit."

"Then why were you baptized?" Paul asked.

They answered, "Because of what John taught."*

Paul replied, "John baptized people so that they would turn to God. But he also told them that someone else was coming, and that they should put their faith in him. Jesus is the one that John was talking about." After the people heard Paul say this, they were baptized in the name of the Lord Jesus. Then Paul placed his hands on them. The Holy Spirit was given to them, and they spoke unknown languages and prophesied. There were about twelve men in this group.

For three months Paul went to the Jewish meeting place and talked bravely with the Jewish people about God's kingdom. He tried to win them over, but some of them were stubborn and refused to believe. In front of everyone they said terrible things about God's Way. Paul left and took the followers with him to the lecture hall of Tyrannus. He spoke there every day for two years, until every Jew and Gentile* in Asia had heard the Lord's message.

The Sons of Sceva
(Acts 19.11-20)

God gave Paul the power to work great miracles. People even took handkerchiefs and aprons that had touched Paul's body, and they carried them to everyone who was sick. All of the sick people were healed, and the evil spirits went out.

Some Jewish men started going around trying to force out evil spirits by using the name of the Lord Jesus. They said to the spirits, "Come out in the name of that same Jesus that Paul preaches about!"

Seven sons of a Jewish high priest named Sceva were doing this, when an evil spirit said to them, "I know Jesus! And I have heard about Paul. But who are you?" Then the man with the evil spirit jumped on them and beat them up. They ran out of the house, naked and bruised.

All the Jews and Gentiles* in Ephesus heard about this. They were so frightened that they praised the name of the Lord Jesus. Many who were followers now started telling everyone about the evil things they had been doing. Some who had been practicing witchcraft even brought their books and burned them in public. These books were worth about fifty thousand silver coins. So the Lord's message spread and became even more powerful.

The Riot in Ephesus
(Acts 19.21-41)

After all of this had happened, Paul decided* to visit Macedonia and Achaia on his way to Jerusalem. Paul had said, "From there I will go on to Rome." So he sent his two helpers, Timothy and Erastus, to Macedonia. But he stayed on in Asia for a while.

At that time there was serious trouble because of the Lord's Way.* A silversmith named Demetrius had a business that made silver models of the temple of the goddess Artemis. Those who worked for him earned a lot of money. Demetrius brought together everyone who was in the same business and said:

> Friends, you know that we make a good living at this. But you have surely seen and heard how this man Paul is upsetting a lot of people, not only in Ephesus, but almost everywhere in Asia. He claims that the gods we humans make are not really gods at all. Everyone will start saying terrible things about

our business. They will stop respecting the temple of the goddess Artemis, who is worshiped in Asia and all over the world. Our great goddess will be forgotten!

When the workers heard this, they got angry and started shouting, "Great is Artemis, the goddess of the Ephesians!" Soon the whole city was in a riot, and some men grabbed Gaius and Aristarchus, who had come from Macedonia with Paul. Then everyone in the crowd rushed to the place where the town meetings were held.

Paul wanted to go out and speak to the people, but the Lord's followers would not let him. A few of the local officials were friendly to Paul, and they sent someone to warn him not to go.

Some of the people in the meeting were shouting one thing, and others were shouting something else. Everyone was completely confused, and most of them did not even know why they were there.

Several of the Jewish leaders pushed a man named Alexander to the front of the crowd and started telling him what to say. He motioned with his hand and tried to explain what was going on. But when the crowd saw that he was Jewish, they all shouted for two hours, "Great is Artemis, the goddess of the Ephesians!"

Finally, a town official made the crowd be quiet. Then he said:

People of Ephesus, who in the world does not know that our city is the center for worshiping the great goddess Artemis? Who does not know that her image which fell from heaven is right here? No one can deny this, and so you should calm down and not do anything foolish. You have brought men in here who have not robbed temples or spoken against our goddess.

If Demetrius and his workers have a case against these men, we have courts and judges. Let them take their complaints there. But if you want to do more than that, the matter will have to be brought before the city council. We could easily be accused of starting a riot today. There is no excuse for it! We cannot even give a reason for this uproar.

After saying this, he told the people to leave.

Paul Goes Through Macedonia and Greece
(Acts 20.1-6)

When the riot was over, Paul sent for the followers and encouraged them. He then told them good-by and left for Macedonia. As he traveled from place to place, he encouraged the followers with many messages. Finally, he went to Greece* and stayed there for three months.

Paul was about to sail to Syria. But some of the Jewish leaders plotted against him, so he decided to return by way of Macedonia. With him were Sopater, son of Pyrrhus from Berea, and Aristarchus and Secundus from Thessalonica. Gaius from Derbe was also with him, and so were Timothy and the two Asians, Tychicus and Trophimus. They went on ahead to Troas and waited for us there. After the Festival of Thin Bread, we sailed from Philippi. Five days later we met them in Troas and stayed there for a week.

Paul's Last Visit to Troas
(Acts 20.7-12)

On the first day of the week* we met to worship and to break bread together.* Paul spoke to the people until midnight because he was leaving the next morning. In the

upstairs room where we were meeting, there were a lot of lamps. A young man by the name of Eutychus was sitting on a window sill. While Paul was speaking, the young man got very sleepy. Finally, he went to sleep and fell three floors all the way down to the ground. When they picked him up, he was dead.

Paul went down and bent over Eutychus. He took him in his arms and said, "Don't worry! He's alive." After Paul had gone back upstairs, he broke bread, and ate with us. He then spoke until dawn and left. Then the followers took the young man home alive and were very happy.

The Voyage from Troas to Miletus
(Acts 20.13-16)

Paul decided to travel by land to Assos. The rest of us went on ahead by ship, and we were to take him aboard there. When he met us in Assos, he came aboard, and we sailed on to Mitylene. The next day we came to a place near Chios, and the following day we reached Samos. The day after that we sailed to Miletus. Paul had decided to sail on past Ephesus, because he did not want to spend too much time in Asia. He was in a hurry and wanted to be in Jerusalem in time for Pentecost.*

Paul Says Good-by to the Church Leaders of Ephesus

(Acts 20.17-38)

From Miletus Paul sent a message for the church leaders at Ephesus to come and meet with him. When they got there, he said:

You know everything I did during the time I was with you when I first came to Asia. Some of the Jews plotted against me and caused me a lot of sorrow and trouble. But I served the Lord and was humble. When I preached in public or taught in your homes, I didn't hold back from telling anything that would help you. I told Jews and Gentiles to turn to God and have faith in our Lord Jesus.

I don't know what will happen to me in Jerusalem, but I must obey God's Spirit and go there. In every city that I visit, the Holy Spirit tells me I will be put in jail and will be in trouble in Jerusalem. But I don't care what happens to me, as long as I finish the work that the Lord Jesus gave me to do. And that work is to tell the good news about God's great kindness.

I have gone from place to place, preaching to you about God's kingdom, but now I know that none of you will ever see me again. I tell you today that I am no longer responsible for any of you! I have told you everything that God wants you to know. Look after yourselves and everyone the Holy Spirit has placed in your care. Be like shepherds to God's church. It is the flock that he bought with the blood of his own Son.*

I know that after I am gone, others will come like fierce wolves to attack you. Some of your own people will tell lies to win over the Lord's followers. Be on your guard! Remember how day and night for three years I kept warning you with tears in my eyes.

I now place you in God's care. Remember the message about his great kindness! This message can help you and give you what belongs to you as God's people. I have never wanted anyone's money or clothes. You know how I have worked with my own hands to make a living for myself and my friends. By everything I did, I showed how you should work to help everyone who is weak. Remember that our Lord Jesus said, "More blessings come from giving than from receiving."

After Paul had finished speaking, he kneeled down with all of them and prayed. Everyone cried and hugged

and kissed him. They were especially sad because Paul had told them, "You will never see me again."

Then they went with him to the ship.

Paul Goes to Jerusalem
(Acts 21.1-16)

After saying good-by, we sailed straight to Cos. The next day we reached Rhodes and from there sailed on to Patara. We found a ship going to Phoenicia, so we got on board and sailed off.

We came within sight of Cyprus and then sailed south of it on to the port of Tyre in Syria. The ship was going to unload its cargo there. We looked up the Lord's followers and stayed with them for a week. The Holy Spirit had told them to warn Paul not to go on to Jerusalem. But when the week was over, we started on our way again. All the men, together with their wives and children, walked with us from the town to the seashore. We kneeled on the beach and prayed. Then after saying good-by to each other, we got into the ship, and they went back home.

We sailed from Tyre to Ptolemais, where we greeted the followers and stayed with them for a day. The next day we went to Caesarea and stayed with Philip, the preacher. He was one of the seven men who helped the apostles, and he had four unmarried* daughters who prophesied.

We had been in Caesarea for several days, when the prophet Agabus came to us from Judea. He took Paul's belt, and with it he tied up his own hands and feet. Then he told us, "The Holy Spirit says that some of the Jewish leaders in Jerusalem will tie up the man who owns this belt. They will also hand him over to the Gentiles." After Agabus said this, we and the followers living there begged Paul not to go to Jerusalem.

But Paul answered, "Why are you crying and breaking my heart? I am not only willing to be put in jail for the Lord Jesus. I am even willing to die for him in Jerusalem!"

Since we could not get Paul to change his mind, we gave up and said, "Lord, please make us willing to do what you want."

Then we got ready to go to Jerusalem. Some of the followers from Caesarea went with us and took us to stay in the home of Mnason. He was from Cyprus and had been a follower from the beginning.

Paul Visits James
(Acts 21.17-26)

When we arrived in Jerusalem, the Lord's followers gladly welcomed us. Paul went with us to see James* the next day, and all the church leaders were present. Paul greeted them and told how God had used him to help the Gentiles. Everyone who heard this praised God and said to Paul:

My friend, you can see how many tens of thousands of the Jewish people have become followers! And all of them are eager to obey the Law of Moses. But they have been told that you are teaching those who live among the Gentiles to disobey this Law. They claim that you are telling them not to circumcise their sons or to follow Jewish customs.

What should we do now that our people have heard that you are here? Please do what we ask, because four of our men have made special promises to God. Join with them and prepare yourself for the ceremony that goes with the promises. Pay the cost for their heads to be shaved. Then everyone will learn that the reports about you are not true. They will know that you do obey the Law of Moses.

Some while ago we told the Gentile followers what we think they should do. We instructed them not to eat anything offered to idols. They were told not to eat any meat with blood still in it or the meat of an animal that has been strangled. They were also told not to commit any terrible sexual sins.*

The next day Paul took the four men with him and got himself ready at the same time they did. Then he went into the temple and told when the final ceremony would take place and when an offering would be made for each of them.

Paul Is Arrested
(Acts 21.27-36)

When the period of seven days for the ceremony was almost over, some of the Jewish people from Asia saw Paul in the temple. They got a large crowd together and started attacking him. They were shouting, "Friends, help us! This man goes around everywhere, saying bad things about our nation and about the Law of Moses and about this temple.

He has even brought shame to this holy temple by bringing in Gentiles." Some of them thought that Paul had brought Trophimus from Ephesus into the temple, because they had seen them together in the city.

The whole city was in an uproar, and the people turned into a mob. They grabbed Paul and dragged him out of the temple. Then suddenly the doors were shut. The people were about to kill Paul when the Roman army commander heard that all Jerusalem was starting to riot. So he quickly took some soldiers and officers and ran to where the crowd had gathered.

As soon as the mob saw the commander and soldiers, they stopped beating Paul. The army commander went over and arrested him and had him bound with two chains. Then he tried to find out who Paul was and what he had done. Part of the crowd shouted one thing, and part of them shouted something else. But they were making so much noise that the commander could not find out a thing. Then he ordered Paul to be taken into the fortress. As they reached the steps, the crowd became so wild that the soldiers had to lift Paul up and carry him. The crowd followed and kept shouting, "Kill him! Kill him!"

Paul Speaks to the Crowd
(Acts 21.37—22.23)

When Paul was about to be taken into the fortress, he asked the commander, "Can I say something to you?"

"How do you know Greek?" the commander asked. "Aren't you that Egyptian who started a riot not long ago and led four thousand terrorists into the desert?"

"No!" Paul replied. "I am a Jew from Tarsus, an important city in Cilicia. Please let me speak to the crowd."

The commander told him he could speak, so Paul

stood on the steps and motioned to the people. When they were quiet, he spoke to them in Aramaic:

"My friends and leaders of our nation, listen as I explain what happened!" When the crowd heard Paul speak to them in Aramaic, they became even quieter. Then Paul said:

I am a Jew, born and raised in the city of Tarsus in Cilicia. I was a student of Gamaliel and was taught to follow every single law of our ancestors. In fact, I was just as eager to obey God as any of you are today.

I made trouble for everyone who followed the Lord's Way,* and I even had some of them killed. I had others arrested and put in jail. I didn't care if they were men or women. The high priest and all the council members can tell you that this is true. They even gave me letters to the Jewish leaders in

Damascus, so that I could arrest people there and bring them to Jerusalem to be punished.

One day about noon I was getting close to Damascus, when a bright light from heaven suddenly flashed around. I fell to the ground and heard a voice asking me, "Saul, Saul, why are you so cruel to me?"

"Who are you?" I answered.

The Lord replied, "I am Jesus from Nazareth! I am the one you are so cruel to." The men who were traveling with me saw the light, but did not hear the voice.

I asked, "Lord, what do you want me to do?"

Then he told me, "Get up and go to Damascus. When you get there, you will be told what to do." The light had been so bright that I couldn't see. And the other men had to lead me by the hand to Damascus.

In that city there was a man named Ananias, who faithfully obeyed the Law of Moses and was well liked by all the Jewish people living there. He came to me and said, "Saul, my friend, you can now see again!"

At once I could see. Then Ananias told me, "The God that our ancestors worshiped has chosen you to know what he wants done. He has chosen you to see the One Who Obeys God* and to hear his voice. You must tell everyone what you have seen and heard. What are you waiting for? Get up! Be baptized, and wash away your sins by praying to the Lord."

After this I returned to Jerusalem and went to the temple to pray. There I had a vision of the Lord who said to me, "Hurry and leave Jerusalem! The people will not listen to what you say about me."

I replied, "Lord, they know that in many of our meeting places I arrested and beat people who had faith in you. Stephen was killed because he spoke for you, and I stood there and cheered them on. I even guarded the clothes of the men who murdered him."

But the Lord told me to go, and he promised to send me far away to the Gentiles.

The crowd listened until Paul said this. Then they started shouting, "Get rid of this man! He doesn't deserve to live." They kept shouting. They waved their clothes around and threw dust into the air.

Paul and the Roman Army Commander
(Acts 22.24-29)

The Roman commander ordered Paul to be taken into the fortress and beaten with a whip. He did this to find out why the people were screaming at Paul.

While the soldiers were tying Paul up to be beaten, he asked the officer standing there, "Is it legal to beat a Roman citizen before he has been tried in court?"

When the officer heard this, he went to the commander and said, "What are you doing? This man is a Roman citizen!"

The commander went to Paul and asked, "Tell me, are you a Roman citizen?"

"Yes," Paul answered.

The commander then said, "I paid a lot of money to become a Roman citizen."*

But Paul replied, "I was born a Roman citizen."

The men who were about to beat and question Paul quickly backed off. And the commander himself was frightened when he realized that he had put a Roman citizen in chains.

Paul Is Tried by the Council
(Acts 22.30—23.11)

The next day the commander wanted to know the real reason why the Jewish leaders had brought charges against Paul. So he had Paul's chains removed, and he ordered the chief priests and the whole council to meet. Then he had Paul led in and made him stand in front of them.

Paul looked straight at the council members and said, "My friends, to this day I have served God with a clear conscience!"

Then Ananias the high priest ordered the men standing beside Paul to hit him on the mouth. Paul turned to the high priest and said, "You whitewashed wall!* God will hit you. You sit there to judge me by the Law of Moses. But at the same time you order men to break the Law by hitting me."

The men standing beside Paul asked, "Don't you know you are insulting God's high priest?"

Paul replied, "Oh! I didn't know he was the high priest. The Scriptures do tell us not to speak evil about a leader of our people."

When Paul saw that some of the council members were Sadducees and others were Pharisees, he shouted, "My friends, I am a Pharisee and the son of a Pharisee. I am on trial simply because I believe that the dead will be raised to life."

As soon as Paul said this, the Pharisees and the Sadducees got into a big argument, and the council members started taking sides. The Sadducees do not believe in angels or spirits or that the dead will rise to life. But the Pharisees believe in all of these, and so there was a lot of shouting. Some of the teachers of the Law of Moses were Pharisees. Finally, they became angry and said, "We don't find anything wrong with this man. Maybe a spirit or an angel really did speak to him."

The argument became fierce, and the commander was afraid that Paul would be pulled apart. So he ordered the soldiers to go in and rescue Paul. Then they took him back into the fortress.

That night the Lord stood beside Paul and said, "Don't worry! Just as you have told others about me in Jerusalem, you must also tell about me in Rome."

A Plot to Kill Paul
(Acts 23.12-22)

The next morning more than forty Jewish men got together and vowed that they would not eat or drink anything until they had killed Paul. Then some of them went to the chief priests and the nation's leaders and said, "We have promised God that we would not eat a thing until we have killed Paul. You and everyone in the council must go to the commander and pretend that you want to find out more about the charges against Paul. Ask for him to be brought before your court. Meanwhile, we will be waiting to kill him before he gets there."

When Paul's nephew heard about the plot, he went to the fortress and told Paul about it. So Paul said to one of

the army officers, "Take this young man to the commander. He has something to tell him."

The officer took the young man to the commander and said, "The prisoner named Paul asked me to bring this young man to you, because he has something to tell you."

The commander took the young man aside and asked him in private, "What do you want to tell me?"

He answered, "Some men are planning to ask you to bring Paul down to the Jewish council tomorrow. They will claim that they want to find out more about him. But please don't do what they say. More than forty men are going to attack Paul. They have made a vow not to eat or drink anything until they have killed him. Even now they are waiting to hear what you decide."

The commander sent the young man away after saying to him, "Don't let anyone know that you told me this."

Paul Is Sent to Felix the Governor

(Acts 23.23-35)

The commander called in two of his officers and told them, "By nine o'clock tonight have two hundred soldiers ready to go to Caesarea. Take along seventy men on horseback and two hundred foot soldiers with spears. Get a

horse ready for Paul and make sure that he gets safely through to Felix the governor."

The commander wrote a letter that said:

Greetings from Claudius Lysias to the Honorable Governor Felix:

Some Jews grabbed this man and were about to kill him. But when I found out that he was a Roman citizen, I took some soldiers and rescued him.

I wanted to find out what they had against him. So I brought him before their council and learned that the charges concern only their Jewish laws. This man is not guilty of anything for which he should die or even be put in jail.

As soon as I learned that there was a plot against him, I sent him to you and told their leaders to bring charges against him in your court.

The soldiers obeyed the commander's orders, and that same night they took Paul to the city of Antipatris. The next day the foot soldiers returned to the fortress and let the soldiers on horseback take him the rest of the way. When they came to Caesarea, they gave the letter to the governor and handed Paul over to him.

The governor read the letter. Then he asked Paul and found out that he was from Cilicia. The governor said, "I will listen to your case as soon as the people come to bring their charges against you." After saying this, he gave orders for Paul to be kept as a prisoner in Herod's palace.*

Paul Is Accused in the Court of Felix
(Acts 24.1-9)

Five days later Ananias the high priest, together with the Jewish leaders and a lawyer named Tertullus, went to the governor to present their case against Paul. So Paul was called in, and Tertullus stated the case against him:*

> Honorable Felix, you have brought our people a long period of peace, and because of your concern our nation is much better off. All of us are always grateful for what you have done. I don't want to bother you, but please be patient with us and listen to me for just a few minutes.

> This man has been found to be a real pest and troublemaker for Jews all over the world. He is also a leader of a group called Nazarenes. When he tried to disgrace the temple, we arrested him.* If you question him, you will find out for yourself that all our charges are true.

The Jewish crowd spoke up and agreed with what Tertullus had said.

Paul Defends Himself
(Acts 24.10-23)

The governor motioned for Paul to speak, and he began:

> I know that you have judged the people of our nation for many years, and I am glad to defend myself in your court.

> It was no more than twelve days ago that I went to worship in Jerusalem. You can find this out easily enough. Never once did the Jews find me arguing with anyone in the temple. I didn't cause

trouble in the Jewish meeting places or in the city itself. There is no way that they can prove these charges that they are now bringing against me.

I admit that the Jewish leaders think that the Lord's Way* which I follow is based on wrong beliefs. But I still worship the same God that my ancestors worshiped. And I believe everything written in the Law of Moses and in the Prophets.* I am just as sure as these people are that God will raise from death everyone who is good or evil. And because I am sure, I try my best to have a clear conscience in whatever I do for God or for people.

After being away for several years, I returned here to bring gifts for the poor people of my nation and to offer sacrifices. This is what I was doing when I was found going through a ceremony in the temple. I was not with a crowd, and there was no uproar.

Some Jews from Asia were there at that time, and if they have anything to say against me, they should be here now. Or ask the ones who are here. They can tell you that they didn't find me guilty of anything when I was tried by their own council. The only charge they can bring against me is what I shouted out in court, when I said, "I am on trial today because I believe that the dead will be raised to life!"

Felix knew a lot about the Lord's Way.* But he brought the trial to an end and said, "I will make my

decision after Lysias the commander arrives." He then ordered the army officer to keep Paul under guard, but not to lock him up or to stop his friends from helping him.

Paul Is Kept Under Guard
(Acts 24.24-27)

Several days later Felix and his wife Drusilla, who was Jewish, went to the place where Paul was kept under guard. They sent for Paul and listened while he spoke to them about having faith in Christ Jesus. But Felix was frightened when Paul started talking to them about doing right, about self-control, and about the coming judgment. So he said to Paul, "That's enough for now. You may go. But when I have time I will send for you." After this, Felix often sent for Paul and talked with him, because he hoped that Paul would offer him a bribe.

Two years later Porcius Festus became governor in place of Felix. But since Felix wanted to do the Jewish leaders a favor, he kept Paul in jail.

Paul Asks to Be Tried by the Roman Emperor
(Acts 25.1-12)

Three days after Festus had become governor, he went from Caesarea to Jerusalem. There the chief priests and the Jewish leaders told him about their charges against Paul. They also asked Festus if he would be willing to bring Paul to Jerusalem. They begged him to do this because they were planning to attack and kill Paul on the way. But Festus told them, "Paul will be kept in Caesarea, and I am soon going there myself. If he has done anything wrong, let your leaders go with me and bring charges against him there."

Festus stayed in Jerusalem for eight or ten more days before going to Caesarea. Then the next day he took his place as judge and had Paul brought into court. As soon as Paul came in, the Jewish leaders from Jerusalem crowded around him and said he was guilty of many serious crimes. But they could not prove anything. Then Paul spoke in his own defense, "I have not broken the Law of my people. And I have not done anything against either the temple or the Emperor."

Festus wanted to please the Jewish leaders. So he asked Paul, "Are you willing to go to Jerusalem and be tried by me on these charges?"

Paul replied, "I am on trial in the Emperor's court, and that's where I should be tried. You know very well that I have not done anything to harm the Jewish nation. If I had done something deserving death, I would not ask to escape the death penalty. But I am not guilty of any of these crimes, and no one has the right to hand me over to these Jews. I now ask to be tried by the Emperor himself."

After Festus had talked this over with members of his council, he told Paul, "You have asked to be tried by the Emperor, and to the Emperor you will go!"

Paul Speaks to Agrippa and Bernice
(Acts 25.13-27)

A few days later King Agrippa and Bernice came to Caesarea to visit Festus. They had been there for several days, when Festus told the king about the charges against Paul. He said:

> Felix left a man here in jail, and when I went to Jerusalem, the chief priests and the Jewish leaders came and asked me to find him guilty. I told them that it is not the Roman custom to hand a man over

to people who are bringing charges against him. He must first have the chance to meet them face to face and to defend himself against their charges.

So when they came here with me, I wasted no time. On the very next day I took my place on the judge's bench and ordered him to be brought in. But when the men stood up to make their charges against him, they did not accuse him of any of the crimes that I thought they would. Instead, they argued with him about some of their Jewish beliefs and about a dead man named Jesus, who Paul said was alive.

Since I did not know how to find out the truth about all this, I asked Paul if he would be willing to go to Jerusalem and be put on trial there. But Paul asked to be kept in jail until the Emperor could decide his case. So I ordered him to be kept here until I could send him to the Emperor.

Then Agrippa said to Festus, "I would also like to hear what this man has to say."

Festus answered, "You can hear him tomorrow."

The next day Agrippa and Bernice made a big show as they came into the meeting room. High ranking army officers and leading citizens of the town were also there. Festus then ordered Paul to be brought in and said:

King Agrippa and other guests, look at this man! Every Jew from Jerusalem and Caesarea has come to me, demanding for him to be put to death. I have not found him guilty of any crime deserving death. But because he has asked to be judged by the Emperor, I have decided to send him to Rome.

I have to write some facts about this man to the Emperor. So I have brought him before all of you, but especially before you, King Agrippa. After we have talked about his case, I will then have something to write. It makes no sense to send a prisoner to the Emperor without stating the charges against him.

Paul's Defense before Agrippa
(Acts 26.1-32)

Agrippa told Paul, "You may now speak for yourself." Paul stretched out his hand and said:

King Agrippa, I am glad for this chance to defend myself before you today on all these charges that my own people have brought against me. You know a lot about our Jewish customs and the beliefs that divide us. So I ask you to listen patiently to me.

All the Jews have known me since I was a child. They know what kind of life I have lived in my

own country and in Jerusalem. If they were willing, they could tell you that I was a Pharisee, a member of a group that is more strict than any other. Now I am on trial because I believe the promise that God made to our people long ago.

Day and night our twelve tribes have earnestly served God, waiting for his promised blessings. King Agrippa, because of this hope, the Jewish leaders have brought charges against me. Why should any of you doubt that God raises the dead to life?

I once thought that I should do everything I could to oppose Jesus from Nazareth. I did this first in Jerusalem, and with the authority of the chief priests I put many of God's people in jail. I even voted for them to be killed. I often had them punished in our meeting places, and I tried to make them give up their faith. In fact, I was so angry with them, that I went looking for them in foreign cities.

King Agrippa, one day I was on my way to Damascus with the authority and permission of the chief priests. About noon I saw a light brighter than the sun. It flashed from heaven on me and on everyone traveling with me. We all fell to the ground. Then I heard a voice say to me in Aramaic, "Saul, Saul, why are you so cruel to me? It's foolish to fight against me!"

"Who are you?" I asked.

Then the Lord answered, "I am Jesus! I am the one you are so cruel to. Now stand up. I have appeared to you, because I have chosen you to be my servant. You are to tell others what you have learned about me and what I will show you later."

The Lord also said, "I will protect you from the

Jews and from the Gentiles that I am sending you to. I want you to open their eyes, so that they will turn from darkness to light and from the power of Satan to God. Then their sins will be forgiven, and by faith in me they will become part of God's holy people."

King Agrippa, I obeyed this vision from heaven. First I preached to the people in Damascus, and then I went to Jerusalem and all over Judea. Finally, I went to the Gentiles and said, "Stop sinning and turn to God! Then prove what you have done by the way you live."

That is why the Jews grabbed me in the temple and tried to kill me. But all this time God has helped me, and I have preached both to the rich and to the poor. I have told them only what the prophets and Moses said would happen. I told them how the Messiah would suffer and be the first to be raised from death, so that he could bring light to his own people and to the Gentiles.

Before Paul finished defending himself, Festus shouted, "Paul, you're crazy! Too much learning has driven you out of your mind."

But Paul replied, "Honorable Festus, I am not crazy. What I am saying is true, and it makes sense. None of these things happened off in a corner somewhere. I am sure that King Agrippa knows what I am talking about. That's why I can speak so plainly to him."

Then Paul said to Agrippa, "Do you believe what the prophets said? I know you do."

Agrippa asked Paul, "In such a short time do you think you can talk me into being a Christian?"

Paul answered, "Whether it takes a short time or a long time, I wish you and everyone else who hears me today would become just like me! Except, of course, for these chains."

Then King Agrippa, Governor Festus, Bernice, and everyone who was with them got up. But before they left, they said, "This man is not guilty of anything. He doesn't deserve to die or to be put in jail."

Agrippa told Festus, "Paul could have been set free, if he had not asked to be tried by the Roman Emperor."

Paul Is Taken to Rome

(Acts 27.1-12)

When it was time for us to sail to Rome, Captain Julius from the Emperor's special troops was put in charge of Paul and the other prisoners. We went aboard a ship from Adramyttium that was about to sail to some ports along the coast of Asia. Aristarchus from Thessalonica in Macedonia sailed on the ship with us.

The next day we came to shore at Sidon. Captain Julius was very kind to Paul. He even let him visit his friends, so they could give him whatever he needed. When we left Sidon, the winds were blowing against us, and we sailed close to the island of Cyprus to be safe from the wind. Then we sailed south of Cilicia and Pamphylia until we came to the port of Myra in Lycia. There the army captain

found a ship from Alexandria that was going to Italy. So he ordered us to board that ship.

We sailed along slowly for several days and had a hard time reaching Cnidus. The wind would not let us go any farther in that direction, so we sailed past Cape Salmone, where the island of Crete would protect us from the wind. We went slowly along the coast and finally reached a place called Fair Havens, not far from the town of Lasea.

By now we had already lost a lot of time, and sailing was no longer safe. In fact, even the Day of Atonement* was past. Then Paul spoke to the crew of the ship, "Men, listen to me! If we sail now, our ship and its cargo will be badly damaged, and many lives will be lost." But Julius listened to the captain of the ship and its owner, rather than to Paul.

The harbor at Fair Havens was not a good place to spend the winter. Because of this, almost everyone agreed that we should at least try to sail along the coast of Crete as far as Phoenix. It had a harbor that opened toward the southwest and northwest,* and we could spend the winter there.

The Storm at Sea
(Acts 27.13-38)

When a gentle wind from the south started blowing, the men thought it was a good time to do what they had planned. So they pulled up the anchor, and we sailed along the coast of Crete. But soon a strong wind called "The Northeaster" blew against us from the island. The wind struck the ship, and we could not sail against it. So we let the wind carry the ship.

We went along the island of Cauda on the side that

was protected from the wind. We had a hard time holding the lifeboat in place, but finally we got it where it belonged. Then the sailors wrapped ropes around the ship to hold it together. They lowered the sail and let the ship drift along, because they were afraid it might hit the sandbanks in the gulf of Syrtis.

The storm was so fierce that the next day they threw some of the ship's cargo overboard. Then on the third day, with their bare hands they threw overboard some of the ship's gear. For several days we could not see either the sun or the stars. A strong wind kept blowing, and we finally gave up all hope of being saved.

Since none of us had eaten anything for a long time, Paul stood up and told the men:

You should have listened to me! If you had stayed on in Crete, you would not have had this damage and loss. But now I beg you to cheer up, because you will be safe. Only the ship will be lost.

I belong to God, and I worship him. Last night he sent an angel to tell me, "Paul, don't be afraid! You will stand trial before the Emperor. And because of you, God will save the lives of everyone on the ship." Cheer up! I am sure that God will do exactly what he promised. But we will first be shipwrecked on some island.

For fourteen days and nights we had been blown around over the Mediterranean Sea. But about midnight the sailors realized that we were getting near land. They measured and found that the water was about one hundred and twenty feet deep. A little later they measured again and found it was only about ninety feet. The sailors were afraid that we might hit some rocks, and they let down four

anchors from the back of the ship. Then they prayed for daylight.

The sailors wanted to escape from the ship. So they lowered the lifeboat into the water, pretending that they were letting down an anchor from the front of the ship. But Paul said to Captain Julius and the soldiers, "If the sailors don't stay on the ship, you won't have any chance to save your lives." The soldiers then cut the ropes that held the lifeboat and let it fall into the sea.

Just before daylight Paul begged the people to eat something. He told them, "For fourteen days you have been so worried that you haven't eaten a thing. I beg you to eat something. Your lives depend on it. Do this and not one of you will be hurt."

After Paul had said this, he took a piece of bread and gave thanks to God. Then in front of everyone, he broke the bread and ate some. They all felt encouraged, and each of them ate something. There were 276 people on the ship, and after everyone had eaten, they threw the cargo of wheat into the sea to make the ship lighter.

The Shipwreck
(Acts 27.39-44)

Morning came, and the ship's crew saw a coast that they did not recognize. But they did see a cove with a beach. So they decided to try to run the ship aground on the beach. They cut the anchors loose and let them sink into the sea. At the same time they untied the ropes that were holding

the rudders. Next, they raised the sail at the front of the ship and let the wind carry the ship toward the beach. But it ran aground on a sandbank. The front of the ship stuck firmly in the sand, and the rear was being smashed by the force of the waves.

The soldiers decided to kill the prisoners to keep them from swimming away and escaping. But Captain Julius wanted to save Paul's life, and he did not let the soldiers do what they had planned. Instead, he ordered everyone who could swim to dive into the water and head for shore. Then he told the others to hold on to planks of wood or parts of the ship. At last, everyone safely reached shore.

On the Island of Malta

(Acts 28.1-10)

When we came ashore, we learned that the island was called Malta. The local people were very friendly, and

they welcomed us by building a fire, because it was rainy and cold.

After Paul had gathered some wood and had put it on the fire, the heat caused a snake to crawl out, and it bit him on the hand. When the local people saw the snake hanging from Paul's hand, they said to each other, "This man must be a murderer! He didn't drown in the sea, but the goddess of justice will kill him anyway."

Paul shook the snake off into the fire and was not harmed. The people kept thinking that Paul would either swell up or suddenly drop dead. They watched him for a long time, and when nothing happened to him, they changed their minds and said, "This man is a god."

The governor of the island was named Publius, and he owned some of the land around there. Publius was very friendly and welcomed us into his home for three days. His father was in bed, sick with fever and stomach trouble, and Paul went to visit him. Paul healed the man by praying and placing his hands on him.

After this happened, everyone on the island brought their sick people to Paul, and they were all healed. The people were very respectful to us, and when we sailed, they gave us everything we needed.

From Malta to Rome

(Acts 28.11-15)

Three months later we sailed in a ship that had been docked at Malta for the winter. The ship was from Alexandria in Egypt and was known as "The Twin Gods."* We arrived in Syracuse and stayed for three days. From there we sailed to Rhegium. The next day a south wind began to blow, and two days later we arrived in Puteoli. There we found some of the Lord's followers, who begged us to stay with them. A week later we left for the city of Rome.

Some of the followers in Rome heard about us and came to meet us at the Market of Appius and at the Three Inns. When Paul saw them, he thanked God and was encouraged.

Paul in Rome

(Acts 28.16-31)

We arrived in Rome, and Paul was allowed to live in a house by himself with a soldier to guard him.

Three days after we got there, Paul called together some of the Jewish leaders and said:

My friends, I have never done anything to hurt our people, and I have never gone against the customs of our ancestors. But in Jerusalem I was handed over as a prisoner to the Romans. They looked into the charges against me and wanted to release me. They found that I had not done anything deserving death. The Jewish leaders disagreed, so I asked to be tried by the Emperor.

But I don't have anything to say against my own nation. I am bound by these chains because of what we people of Israel hope for. That's why I have called you here to talk about this hope of ours.

The Jewish leaders replied, "No one from Judea has written us a letter about you. And not one of them has come here to report on you or to say anything against you. But we would like to hear what you have to say. We understand that people everywhere are against this new group."

They agreed on a time to meet with Paul, and many of them came to his house. From early morning until late in the afternoon, Paul talked to them about God's kingdom. He used the Law of Moses and the Books of the Prophets* to try to win them over to Jesus.

Some of the Jewish leaders agreed with what Paul said, but others did not. Since they could not agree among themselves, they started leaving. But Paul said, "The Holy Spirit said the right thing when he sent Isaiah the prophet to tell our ancestors,

'Go to these people
       and tell them:
You will listen and listen,
       but never understand.
You will look and look,
       but never see.
All of you
       have stubborn hearts.

Your ears are stopped up,
        and your eyes are covered.
You cannot see or hear
        or understand.
If you could,
you would turn to me,
        and I would heal you.' "

Paul said, "You may be sure that God wants to save the Gentiles! And they will listen."*

For two years Paul stayed in a rented house and welcomed everyone who came to see him. He bravely preached about God's kingdom and taught about the Lord Jesus Christ, and no one tried to stop him.

NOTES (*)

36	**accepted the Lord's Way:** In the book of Acts, this means to become a follower of the Lord Jesus.
40	**and make up your bed:** Or "and fix something to eat."
41	**at about three o'clock:** Probably while he was praying. See 3.1 and the second note for page 11.
42	**roof:** In Palestine the houses usually had a flat roof. Stairs on the outside led up to the roof, which was made of beams and boards covered with packed earth.
42	**unclean and not fit to eat:** The Law of Moses taught that some foods were not fit to eat.
42	**Three:** Some manuscripts have "two;" one manuscript has "some."
45	**what happened:** Or "the message that went."
46	**unclean and not fit to eat:** See the second note for page 42.
47	**Gentiles:** This translates a Greek word that may mean "people who speak Greek" or "people who live as Greeks do." Here the word seems to mean "people who are not Jews." Some manuscripts have "Greeks," which also seems to mean "people who are not Jews."
48	**when Claudius was Emperor:** A.D. 41-54.
48	**Herod:** Herod Agrippa I, the grandson of Herod the Great.
50	**his angel:** Probably meaning "his guardian angel."
52	**went back to Jerusalem:** Some manuscripts have "left Jerusalem," and others have "went to Antioch."
52	**Herod's:** Herod Antipas, the son of Herod the Great.
52	**going without eating:** The Jews often went without eating as a way of showing how much they loved God. This is also called "fasting."
52	**John:** Whose other name was Mark (12.12,25).
53	**John:** Whose other name was Mark (12.12,25).
54	**the Law and the Prophets:** The Jewish Scriptures, that is, the Old Testament.
54	**took care of:** Some manuscripts have "put up with."
55	**cross:** This translates a Greek word that means "wood," "pole," or "tree."
56	**the Lord:** Some manuscripts have "God."
57	**the Lord:** Some manuscripts have "God."
57	**shook the dust from that place off their feet:** This was a way of showing rejection.
57	**Gentiles:** The Greek text has "Greeks," which probably means people who were not Jews. But it may mean Gentiles who worshiped with the Jews.
59	**Hermes:** The Greeks thought of Hermes as the messenger of the other gods, especially of Zeus, their chief god.
61	**went without eating:** See the third note for page 52.
61	**the work they had now completed:** See 13.1-3.
62	**James:** The Lord's brother.
62	**Simon Peter:** The Greek text has "Simeon," which is another form of the name "Simon." The apostle Peter is meant.
63	**not commit any terrible sexual sins:** This probably refers to the laws about the wrong kind of marriages that are forbidden in Leviticus 18.6-18 or to some serious sexual sin.
64	**Judas Barsabbas:** He may have been a brother of Joseph Barsabbas (see 1.23), but the name "Barsabbas" was often used by the Jewish people.

65	Verse 34, which says that Silas decided to stay on in Antioch, is not in some manuscripts.
65	**had him circumcised . . . Timothy's father was Greek:** Timothy would not have been acceptable to the Jews unless he had been circumcised, and Greeks did not circumcise their sons.
66	**in the first district of Macedonia:** Some manuscripts have "and the leading city of Macedonia."
70	**Roman citizens:** Only a small number of the people living in the Roman Empire were citizens, and they had special rights and privileges.
71	**Gentiles:** See the note for page 47.
72	**Epicureans:** People who followed the teaching of a man named Epicurus, who taught that happiness should be the main goal in life.
72	**Stoics:** Followers of a man named Zeno, who taught that people should learn self-control and be guided by their consciences.
72	**people rising from death:** Or "a goddess named 'Rising from Death.' "
75	**Emperor Claudius had ordered all the Jewish people to leave Rome:** Probably A.D. 49, though it may have been A.D. 41.
76	**Gentiles:** Here the word is "Greeks." But see the note for page 47.
76	**shook the dust from his clothes:** This means the same as shaking dust from the feet. See the second note for page 57.
78	**he had his head shaved:** Paul had promised to be a "Nazarite" for a while. This meant that for the time of the promise, he could not cut his hair or drink wine. When the time was over, he would have to cut his hair and offer a sacrifice to God.
78	**the Lord's Way:** See the note for page 36.
79	**Then why were you baptized? . . . Because of what John taught:** Or "In whose name were you baptized? . . . We were baptized in John's name."
80	**Gentile(s):** The text has "Greek(s)" (see the note for page 47).
81	**Gentile(s):** The text has "Greek(s)" (see the note for page 47).
81	**Paul decided:** Or "Paul was led by the Holy Spirit."
81	**the Lord's Way:** See the note for page 36.
83	**Greece:** Probably Corinth.
83	**On the first day of the week:** Since the Jewish day began at sunset, the meeting would have begun in the evening.
83	**break bread together:** See the first note for page 11.
84	**in time for Pentecost:** The Jewish people liked to be in Jerusalem for this festival. See the note for page 5.
85	**the blood of his own Son:** Or "his own blood."
87	**unmarried:** Or "virgin."
88	**James:** The Lord's brother.
89	**not to commit any terrible sexual sins:** See the note for page 63.
91	**followed the Lord's Way:** See the note for page 36.
92	**One Who Obeys God:** That is, Jesus.
94	**Roman citizen:** See the note for page 70.
94	**whitewashed wall:** Someone who pretends to be good, but really isn't.
97	**Herod's palace:** The palace built by Herod the Great and used by the Roman governors of Palestine.

98	**Paul was called in, and Tertullus stated the case against him:** Or "Tertullus was called in and stated the case against Paul."
98	**we arrested him:** Some manuscripts add, "We wanted to judge him by our own laws. But Lysias the commander took him away from us by force. Then Lysias ordered us to bring our charges against this man in your court."
99	**the Lord's Way:** See the note for page 36.
99	**Law of Moses . . . the Prophets:** The Jewish Scriptures, that is, the Old Testament.
107	**Day of Atonement:** This Jewish festival took place near the end of September. The sailing season was dangerous after the middle of September, and it was stopped completely between the middle of November and the middle of March.
107	**southwest and northwest:** Or "northeast and southeast."
113	**known as "The Twin Gods":** Or "carried on its bow a wooden carving of the Twin Gods." These gods were Castor and Pollux, two of the favorite gods among sailors.
114	**Law of Moses and the Books of the Prophets:** The Jewish Bible, that is, the Old Testament.
115	**And they will listen:** Some manuscripts add, "After Paul said this, the people left, but they got into a fierce argument among themselves."